Walking Historic Galveston

A GUIDE TO ITS NEIGHBORHOODS

Jan Johnson

EAKIN PRESS Waco, Texas

FIRST EDITION

Published in the United States of America
By Eakin Press
A Division of Sunbelt Media, Inc.
P.O. Box 21235 Waco, Texas 76702
e-mail: sales@eakinpress.com
website: www.eakinpress.com

1 2 3 4 5 6 7 8 9
ISBN 978-1-934645-79-6
ISBN 1-934645-79-6
Library of Congress Control Number 2009921363

Contents

Preface

In the early morning hours of Saturday, September 13, 2008, seventy-five percent of Galveston's structures were inundated with two to twelve feet of murky salt water from Galveston Bay, courtesy of Hurricane Ike. No longer had we "dodged the bullet" of nature's fury. This guide was written, photos taken, and maps drawn thirteen months before the Island got "Iked." So, as you take to the streets on foot or bike, in a car or carriage, look to the past with an eye to the city's future. What was will be again, only better. Envision Galveston's future as you explore its historic past.

Acknowledgments

Walking Historic Galveston: A Guide to its Neighborhoods is the city's first practical, comprehensive walking guide for visitors to include portions of nine distinct districts on the Island. This book has been my "brain child" for the last ten years, so writing and researching it was both a "Labor of Love" as well as a challenge.

Fortunately, I did not have to be an "Island unto Myself" in this effort—my heartfelt "Thanks" to the cooperative community of caring friends, colleagues, cheerleaders, countless well-wishers and an understanding Dad.

To begin at the beginning of Galveston's historical renaissance, I want to acknowledge the late Tim Thompson (and others) who spearheaded the movement with John Garner and his Historic American Buildings Survey in 1966-67. Thanks to both of them for hiring my mom, Dorris Johnson, as secretary. The tales she told around the dinner table instilled an interest in my Island heritage as well as its vintage buildings at the impressionable age of thirteen.

To my three "Guardian Angels:" Sally Laney for her gentle push all the way from Florida and Brenda Whynot for her encouragement. Most of all, Gene Bindhammer—my "gentleman friend" and partner, a pair of eyes and legs when none other were available, computer tech, motivator, and photographer who helped me to the get job done, every step of the way (pun intended)!

Many others gave generously of their time, knowledge and resources in the production of my first book. First of all, to all those learned writers and researchers who came before, whether paid professionals, architectural scholars or passionate volunteers—bonded to me by our intrinsic love for Galveston Island and its history, whether BOI's or IBC's. Many of their names are listed in the

Bibliography, but others deserve special recognition: GHF contributors Margaret Doran, Mary Remmers, and Leslie Watts; Jane Chapin and Carlotta Barker for their work on so many neighborhood walk pamphlets; Tim Brookover who, through his creative wordplay and gentle editing, made me a much better writer. Fay Allison, retired English teacher, offered her own insight with heartfelt support.

The many pairs of legs, who literally "walked the walks," and looked over my shoulder with invaluable suggestions: Sharon Tipton, Jane and Sandy Rushing, Charlie and Rose Marie Smith, Ed and Lavinia Bircher and Tony Dabney.

The staff of Rosenberg Library's Galveston–Texas History Center, especially Carol Wood, Mary Hernandez, and Casey Greene.

Members of neighborhood groups: Brenda Donaloio, Lissa Graham Reynolds, Mary Branum, Bill Hynek, Shirley Jackson, Trish McDaniel, Alan and Julia Kamen. In particular, I want to recognize the Cedar Lawn Association for their work on the pamphlet celebrating the subdivision's seventy-fifth anniversary in 2002: Weese Doherty and her eight committee members, and Andrew Loomis. And thanks, too, to those who shared their stories: David Bowers, John Campbell, Juliet Straud, and Linda Strevell.

Galveston City Planner Katie Gorman-Tinnemayer, who wisely advised me on the bureaucracy of historic districts, and map-maker Alan Slay. But most of all, to graphic designer Marshall Bayliss, whose patience and skill created ten maps specific to the publisher's painstaking requirements.

Since a simple "Thank You" is not enough, I'd like to borrow a phrase from Shakespeare's *Twelfth Night* to gratefully acknowledge each and every one of you—

"Thanks and Thanks and EVER Thanks!!"

Introduction

WELCOME TO HISTORIC GALVESTON! The history of the Island, rich with colorful characters, spans 500 years. While much of that "ancient history" remains buried in legend and lore, countless records, carefully preserved over the years, chronicled diverse and definitive human stories. Extant structures, spanning the years from 1838 to 1958, still stand as witness. That history reads like a tale of two cities: the richly decadent, highly Victorian "Queen City of the Gulf" and, after the Great 1900 Storm, the damaged but defiant "Free State of Galveston."

Whether you walk (the preferred mode of exploration), cycle, ride in a carriage, or drive, this book will serve as your practical guide to the city's historic districts, neighborhood by neighborhood, tying what is with what was.

Walking Historic Galveston is not meant as a comprehensive scholarly digest full of mere dry, documented historical and architectural facts. These exist already, for the intellectual in us all. Rather, this guidebook is meant for the "Everyman" who wanders the city streets and wonders "What happened here and to whom?" Viewing them from the outside, you'll read the inside human stories of all those who lived, loved and worked in the unusual buildings that survived them—as many and varied as befitting a much larger community.

Not every street in every historic district is included nor every building listed, but merely the highlights . . . and there are many! Keep in mind that structures are not considered historic until they are at least fifty years old, so no building—either residential or commercial—will be included if it was built after 1958. Also, please remember that many inside stories simply remain unknown, because they have yet to be told, researched or publicly documented, possibly because their buildings are still awaiting rebirth by restoration.

As much as possible, documented facts are presented. In some cases, however, documentation was destroyed or simply disappeared, whether by accident or design. In that case, researchers must rely on personal memories and eyewitness accounts. Please remember, too, that the facts in any book are based on present knowledge. That and/or interpretation of that information can be revised as new knowledge develops over time. While the truth takes precedence, beware the term, "Legend has it . . ." This marker signals one of those refutable "Tour Guide Tales," which, despite their lack of documentation, make interesting, fun, sometimes astoundingly good stories!

Navigating the City

Before you take to the streets, book in hand, to see the sights, you need to know the basics about the city's most pedestrian-friendly checkerboard grid, which is itself a relic from the past.

At its inception, the Galveston City Company hired John D. Groesbeck of Albany, New York, to survey and lay out the new city of Galveston. His original town plan, dated 1838, forms a simple but logical pattern that still applies today at least in the historic East End.

Basically, the streets that run approximately north and south are numbered, while the avenues that run approximately east to west are lettered. Since the city began with its natural harbor to the north, the first letters are found on the port side and the lower numbers began in the east. Beginning at the Causeway (Interstate 45, aka I 45) at 59th Street and traveling east to Seawall Boulevard, Broadway equally splits the city north and south, parallel to both the gulf and the bay. 25th Street, aka Rosenberg, was originally designed as the main north/south thoroughfare, linking the port with the beach. Even though much history exists beyond, *Walking Historic Galveston* will go no further west than 53rd Street, nor north of Broadway after 27th Street.

South of Broadway to the west was considered suburban and rural since it was so far from the Strand central business district.

Groesbeck platted ten-acre outlots, each of which consisted of four regular city blocks. These could either be settled as farms, dairies or plantations, become extra large estates for the wealthiest, or subdivided as the city moved south and west.

For getting around Galveston, two minor difficulties developed—some swear merely to confuse visitors. First of all, they ran out of letters! Actually, when the outlots were cut through east to west, it created "½ streets" which run parallel to their lettered avenues one block to the north. Remember, ½ streets are really full avenues!

The second difficulty (and the perhaps most problematic) occurred when city planners honored prominent city fathers by renaming many of the thoroughfares after them, such as Avenue I which became Sealy Avenue. Originally, 25th Street was called Bath Avenue, but it became Rosenberg just prior to the 1900 Storm. Some city streets were named for their purpose, such as Avenue D which became Market. Avenue A, which was originally known as Water, became Port Industrial and is now Harborside Drive. It actually could have been much worse as Groesbeck's preliminary plat named ALL the streets after everything from Texas heroes, wild life, and world capitals, to different cities, states, and rivers, with little logic, rhyme or reason.

Navigating this Guide

To help walking readers avoid confusion, this guide primarily refers to the streets as numbers (ignoring the names) and the avenues by name, if they have one. The one exception is 25th Street whose number designation is interchanged with Rosenberg. To avoid the walker's further confusion, street signs should reflect both letter or number designation as well as its name. Of particular note, even numbered addresses are found on the north side of the street—the more prestigious side as it could capture southern breezes—with odd on the south side of the street throughout the city.

In *Walking Historic Galveston*, each chapter is named for the historic neighborhood you will wander. Remember that the more official the area, the more information is available about its houses

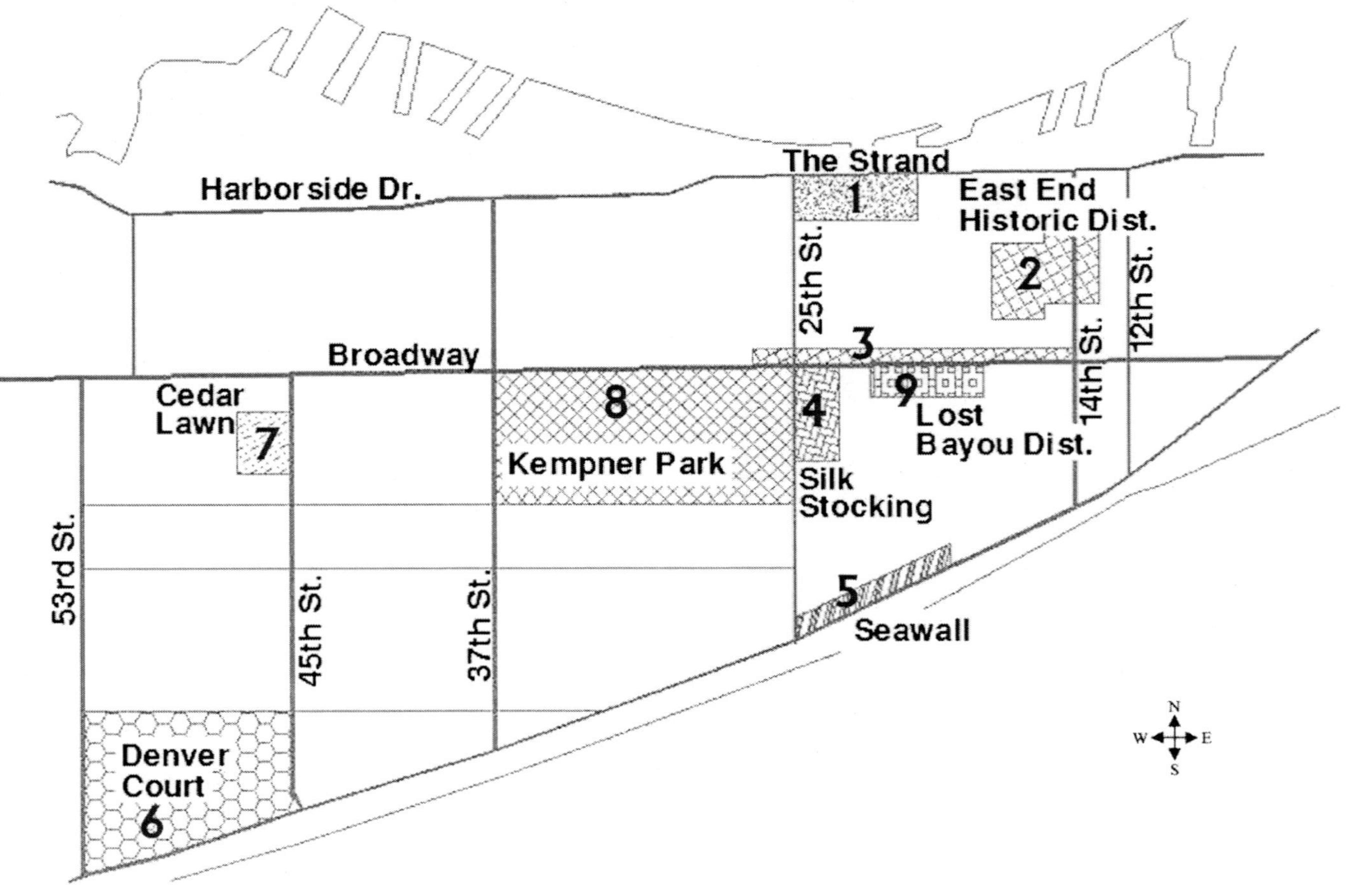

The Strand
1
East End
Historic Dist.
Harborside Dr.
2
25th St.
12th St.
3
14th St.
Broadway
8
9
Lost
Bayou Dist.
Cedar
Lawn
7
4
Kempner Park
Silk
Stocking
5
Seawall
53rd St.
45th St.
37th St.
Denver
Court
6
N
W
E
S

as a matter of public record. Please do not deviate from the route as that may cause some confusion with the text.

Thus far only five Galveston neighborhoods have been officially designated as historic districts and listed as such on the National Register. The Seawall is listed not as a neighborhood but as a kind of park. The Lost Bayou District is a local historic district, while the San Jacinto and Kempner Park Neighborhoods remain local "Districts in Waiting." The chapters are:

Chapter 1—The Strand/Mechanic Strut, the downtown business district which was the first to be nationally recognized in 1970.

Chapter 2—East End Historic District, the residential district which followed five years later. This second chapter is divided into two walks: West Side Wanderings and East Side Stories.

Chapter 3—Broadway Promenade: This main thoroughfare was originally included in the East End District, but this guide devotes a chapter to this "Grand American Avenue."

Chapter 4—Silk Stocking Stroll, another national historic residential district, listed in 1996.

Chapter 5—Seawall Excursion: Created after the 1900 Storm following the Gulf of Mexico shoreline, it is considered an urban parkway with open beaches and public space; a park, by default. You'll complete your excursion while driving to your next walk through the Fort Crockett area.

Chapter 6—Roarin' Twenties Realm—Denver Court. While the first four neighborhoods followed the original Groesbeck city plan, this development from 45th Street to 53rd Street deviated slightly to discourage traffic.

Chapter 7—Cedar Lawn: Against the Grid, which totally disrupted the Groesbeck town plan with its "butterfly" pattern, isolating the elite in a private enclave. Both Denver Court and Cedar Lawn are recognized as national historic districts.

Chapter 8—Roamin' the Kempner Park Neighborhood: This large and diverse neighborhood, south of Broadway and west of 25th Street, is still in the talking stage of protecting its historic integrity, even though the street signs already note its distinction. Purely decoration, they do not signify any official recognition. A small part of the Old Central/Carver Park neighborhood is also included.

Chapter 9—Lost Bayou District, Found: This neighborhood, within the expansive San Jacinto area, received local recognition as historic in 1994 and is protected by the city's Landmark Commission.

Traveling instructions, whether driving to or walking the route, are given in bold type, as are addresses in this practical guide. The numbers at the beginning of each change of direction correlate with the circled numbers on the map to help the walker follow the route properly; they do not denote structures of interest. Maps are provided for every walk, but it may be helpful to carry or refer to a compass at times.

Each chapter begins where the previous walk ended, in sequence, moving east to west then back east after Cedar Lawn—as if the reader planned to do the whole book on a day's outing. If planning your journey into Galveston's past in a more random fashion, please understand that your beginning directions may alter a bit from how and where you choose to approach it.

A few words of caution—on your walk, as you stare up at the lovely buildings, please stay mindful of the walkways. Where there are paved sidewalks, large roots of old live oaks and other trees have resulted in many upheavals over the years. As in any city, please place valuables out of sight, perhaps in the trunk and do not forget to lock your car doors!

Please respect the property and privacy of all residents and homeowners by staying on the public sidewalks. Note that none of the current homeowners are listed—on purpose.

Start exploring the historic districts anywhere you want, following your journey according to your whims. However, *Walking Historic Galveston: A Guide to its Neighborhoods* begins at the source of the city's success: The Strand, next to the only natural harbor west of the Mississippi.

CHAPTER 1

Struttin' on the Strand and Ship Mechanic's Row

DISCOVERED BY SPANIARDS IN THE SIXTEENTH CENTURY and treasured by pirates during the early 1800s, "Galvez Town" grew to become the city of Galveston in 1839 with the promise of its port. Legend has it that 95% of the goods from the East coast and Europe came through Galveston's natural harbor on its way to Texas and the rest of the Southwest. "King Cotton" went out to the rest of the world. Within twenty years, "The Queen City of the Gulf" was crowned the financial center of the state.

Just one block south of the port, the street called The Strand witnessed the prosperity of the city as its central business district, and it became known as "The Wall Street of the Southwest." From the 1840s through 1900, successful merchants erected ornate commercial buildings to reflect their financial good fortune architecturally. Sidewalk canopies, typical of 19th century Texas downtowns, protected customers from the climate.

Today, Galveston's Strand boasts the largest collection of Cast-Iron-Fronted Victorian office buildings in the southern United States. Legend has it that most of this cast iron came to town as ships' ballast. As you explore the district, note that each building boasts a continuing saga, housing boutiques, restaurants and most recently lofts, for both sale and rent. Be aware that over 150 years,

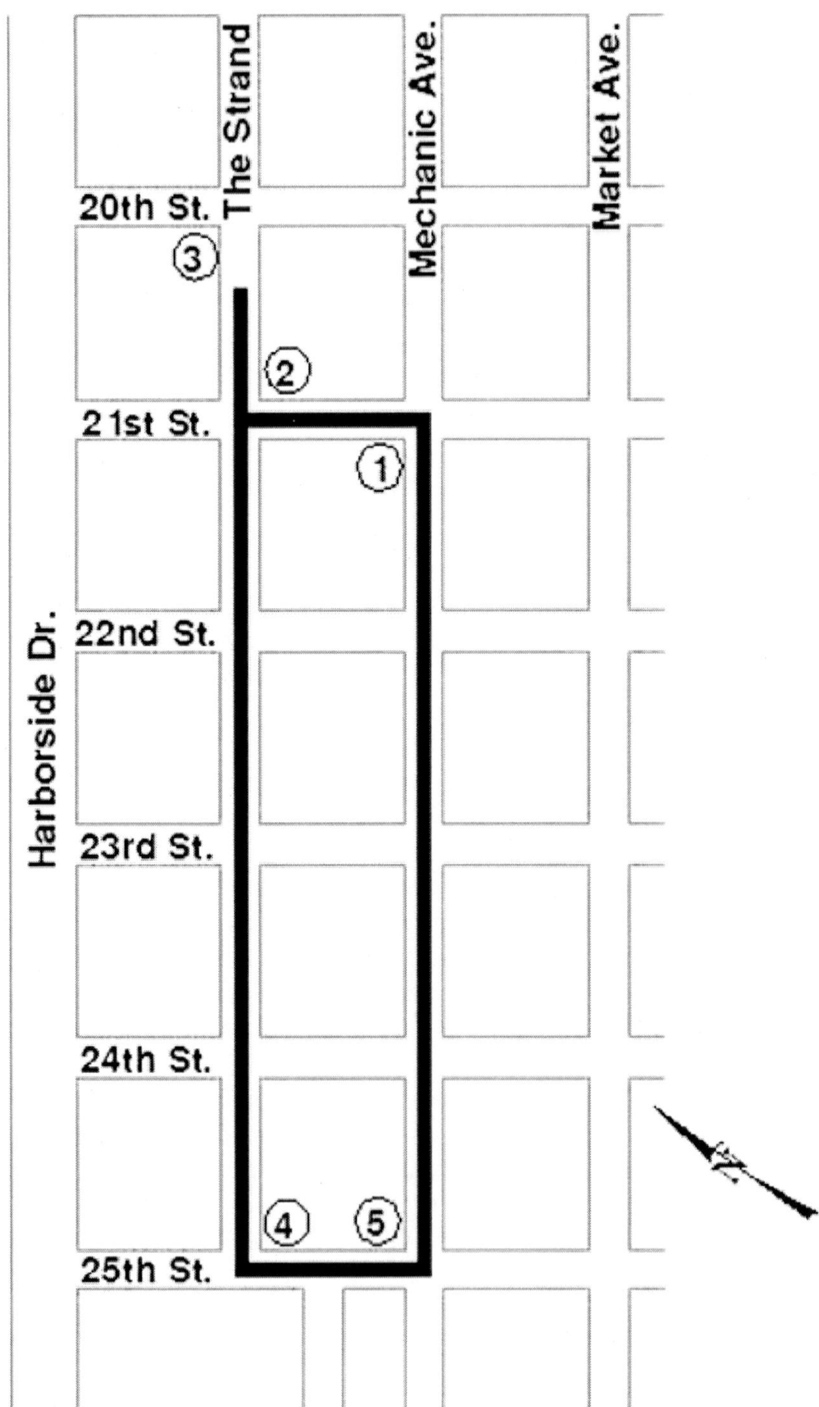
The Strand
Mechanic Ave.
Market Ave.
20th St.
21st St.
22nd St.
23rd St.
24th St.
25th St.
Harborside Dr.
1
2
3
4
5
N

owners either modified addresses or refused to post them at all on their buildings.

Also included in your Strand walk is Ship Mechanic's Row, also known as Mechanic, one block to its south.

▶ ❶ Park your car at 21st Street on Ship Mechanic's Row. If you're not walking on a Sunday, you'll need to "plug" the parking meter. Turn left on 21st Street, walking north to The Strand.

2102 Mechanic Avenue

Ben Milam's austere white block building, trimmed with polished granite, replaced a weighty Victorian building in 1940, as the city's world standing diminished. John Moser's original Galveston Cotton Exchange Building, built in 1879, stood an impressive 3½ stories of red pressed brick trimmed with limestone. It was the first Galveston structure to be featured in a national architectural digest. The reserve of Milam's building sharply contrasts the ornate Victorians in the downtown area.

Original Galveston Cotton Exchange Building

—Courtesy of educator John Glenn

308 21st Street

Catty-cornered across the street, the 11-story Medical Arts building was designed by Scottish architect and engineer, Andrew Fraser in 1929 for W. L. Moody Jr. Note the eight stone faces on the 10th floor. It served as an annex to the original 1913 American National Insurance Company next door, which was demolished in 1972. The tall, white 19-story tower in the background replaced it.

▶ ❷ Turn right on The Strand.

2027 Strand

Appropriately, you'll start your Strand Strut with its oldest buildings. On this corner stands the Jockusch Building, built in 1866 by the Prussiian consul of Galveston.

2025 Strand

Built between 1856 and 1858 by cotton factor and commission merchant Ebenezer B. Nichols, this structure features three different kinds of Boston red brick which was salvaged from ship's ballast.

2021–23 Strand

A 1983 restoration opened the doorways of the 1894 Rogers Building onto the street.

2001–2011 Strand

The Rosenberg Building on the corner was one of three investment properties built by Henry Rosenberg in downtown Galveston during the 1870s. This successful Swiss immigrant was destined to become the city's biggest benefactor even before he died in 1893.

▶ ❸ Cross the avenue and turn left, walking west on the north side of The Strand.

2002-2016 Strand

Construction of Hendley Row began in 1855 by brothers William and Joseph Hendley. With all materials imported from Boston, a total of four adjoining three-story buildings that share a Greek Revival façade were not completed until 1859—just in time for the Civil War. Now missing, its original cupola provided the perfect place to guard Galveston's port. On New Year's Day 1863, the Battle of Galveston was fought here. A sound defeat for Union forces, it secured the state for the Confederate cause. Ironically, that was the same day President Lincoln presented his Emancipation Proclamation which freed only the Southern slaves. It did not take effect in Texas until June 19, 1865, when General Gordon Granger announced it from Union Headquarters at 22nd and Strand. To this day, Texas blacks celebrate Juneteenth. Marked by its grey granite columns, Hendley Row remains the oldest surviving commercial building on the Strand.

Hendley Row

104 21st Street

Across the parking lot stands the Galveston Ice and Cold Storage. Marked on Harborside Drive by a towering smokestack, this commercial building was constructed in 1910, remodeled both in 1912 and 1914. It was reborn as downtown Loft condominiums in 2004. During its conversion, the contractor discovered concrete columns, 24 to 30 inches in diameter, spaced an average of 16 feet apart. Running roof to foundation throughout, this feature created a true "design challenge" for the architects; however, these support columns ensure that this building is going nowhere.

Galveston Ice and Cold Storage

101 21st Street

Directly across 21st Street stands the U.S. Appraisers Building. In 1905, concrete merchant Issac Heffron built a warehouse on this original site of the First and Last Chance Saloon, a popular Victorian watering hole. The appraisers enlarged Heffon's building in 1915.

▶ Cross 21st Street

2002–2004 Strand

At the corner of Strand and 21st Street, knock on the original cast iron columns of the 1890 Adoue-Lobit Commerce Building. They are all that remain of Nicholas Clayton's original Neo-renaissance design.

2101–2107 Strand

Looking across the street, note the pointed arched windows of the Schneider Building, another Clayton design. Ball, Hutchings and Company built it following a fire on June 8, 1877, that destroyed the entire block. The blaze began on Market Avenue and was swept north by a strong southern breeze.

2111 Strand

In 1878, J. Brown and Company built this structure as rental property.

2115 Strand

Next door stands the Oppermann Building, which was designed in 1878 by German- born architect John Moser for the real estate investor, Gustav Oppermann.

2109 Strand

Moser also designed two Strand investments for Clara Lang. This first one was a narrow four-story, which the 1900 Storm reduced to two.

2115 Strand

Sandwiched between the Lang investments, the Marx and Kempner Building once housed a wholesale liquor and cigars supplier.

2117 Strand

Oscar Springer rented Clara Lang's second structure for his German newspaper *Die Galveston Post*. It and the Marx/ Kempner building lost their original cast iron trim during the 1930s. Commissioned by the Galveston Historical Foundation in 1976, New York artist Richard Haas created mural facades to "fool the eye" of casual observers.

2114–16 Strand

You'll pass directly in front of the Mallory Building on the north side of the avenue. Commissioned in 1878 by C. H. Mallory of Baltimore, who founded the steamship company, it served as a warehouse for a provisioning firm owned by his son, David, even though it was named the "Produce Building" for its wholesale grocer tenants. Note its original 14-foot cypress doors. This 1882 building was the first to be restored on The Strand, by Bill Fullen in 1975.

2118–28 Strand

The two-story Mensing Building, built for brothers Gustave and William in 1882, encompasses a full half-block. It originally housed a cotton-factoring firm but, immediately after the 1900 Storm, it served as a morgue. Survivor Hyman Block remembered that his brother "was . . . given a bottle of whiskey" to guard the shrouded naked bodies stacked on the floor. Legend has it that some of their spirits continue to haunt the second-floor loft apartments.

2127 Strand

On the corner across the street, you'll see the First National Bank. This red brick building once housed the oldest chartered bank in Texas. After the 1877 fire destroyed the 1867 P. M. Comegy's original three story design, much of its rich iron ornamentation was salvaged to replicate it. Note its leafy cornices just below the roof and white iron Corinthian columns at the entrance. The original tiled sidewalk was imported from England. The First National Bank now houses the Galveston Arts Center.

▶ **Cross 22nd Street.**

2202–06 Strand

The W. L. Moody Building, another Nicholas Clayton design, was built in 1883 to house the Colonel's cotton commission.

This Neo Renaissance design featured a clock mounted on a cornice above the original fourth floor. In the spring of 1900, that upper story was converted into a fashionable atrium and rooftop garden, which the 1900 Storm winds ripped off on September 8.

2208–10 Strand

According to the current owner, commercial buildings have stood on this site since the late 18th century, when the address was listed as 122 Water Street. Located next to a coal yard to the left, the current structure was built in 1896 and housed the Galveston Hay, Grain and Feed Store. The Moody's atrium landed on top of it during the Great Storm, crushing the three story building to one story. A second story was rebuilt during its repairs. Sign maker Jules Lauve bought it in 1925 and its neighbor at **2212-18**, in 1936. The complex was named after him in 2004 when the ballroom at **2214 Strand** opened upstairs.

2211-23 Strand

The Blum Hardware Company Building dominates the south side of The Strand in this block. A composite of four separate structures, the oldest is the 1858 E. S. Wood Building, closest to 22nd Street, which originally housed a hardware store. Dubbed "The Commercial Row" by John Maxwell Jones in 1857, the next three buildings replaced those destroyed in the fire of June 1877. In 1904, Blum and Company united all four by a uniform façade which amounted to a 90,000 square-foot warehouse for their hardware store until it went out of business four years later. From 1917 to 1966, it housed Black Hardware, when it became Flood and Calvert Marine. It opened as Old Galveston Square in 1986 and still houses a variety of boutiques.

2222–28 Strand

Another building compound stands on the north corner of 23rd and Strand. The three-story 1870 Dragan and Tobyn and Frosh Building survived an 1882 fire. Legend has it that New York railroad magnate Jay Gould had an office on its second floor.

2223–27 Harborside Drive

Behind this building across the alley stands the Thompson and

Company Building. Designed by Nathaniel W. Tobey in 1877 for cotton merchants Wolston, Wells & Vidor, this two-story brick warehouse sold to the Ball, Hutchings & Company just four years later. It continued to change hands over the years until George Mitchell purchased it in 1992. Currently, it is being converted into the Thompson Lofts.

▶ **Continue walking west on the north side of the avenue, crossing 23rd Street which is also known as Tremont.**

Looking right toward the harbor, you might notice the bow of a Carnival cruise ship in port.

Sangerfest Park, a 1994 addition, was named after German men's choral societies which convened on the Island in 1881. Note the mosaic bench compass near the corner which denotes the city's true directions. Behind the park stands the 1916 Armour and Company Building, boasting the best view of Galveston's Port.

Carnival cruise ship in port

2301–07 Strand

Across The Strand on the corner stands the Renaissance Revival Thomas Jefferson League Building. According to the *Galveston Daily News*, the Southern Ornamental Iron Works of New Orleans created the League Buildings' elaborate ironwork. Built in 1872, it once housed a clothing store. A fire on December 2, 1869 destroyed four city blocks of commercial buildings. At that time, the Moro Castle stood on this corner. Some think the fire started during a robbery of the popular saloon on its first floor. Legend has it that volunteer firemen fought the blaze in costume because they had been called from a party in full libation. The whole block was lost but quickly rebuilt the following year, with most of the buildings designed by Comegy and Company.

2309 Strand

Another investment by Henry Rosenberg, this building originally housed the telephone company.

2313 Strand

Liquor wholesaler John Megale hired Comegy's construction supervisor B. O Hamilton to build this structure next door.

2317–19 Strand

This Merchants Mutual Insurance Building replaced a Comegy design also lost in the 1869 fire. According to the *Galveston Daily News*, Hamilton rebuilt it "fac simile." A 1978 restoration replicated its long-lost unique "French" mansard roof, steeply sloped with a central dormer window and small, round portholes on either side.

2323 Strand

Designed by Nicholas Clayton in 1877, the Bolton Estate Building was restored as a popular confectionary in 1976.

2310–14 Strand

Continuing your walk on the north side of the street, the Greenleve, Block and Company building, designed in 1882 by Nicholas Clayton, served as a wholesale store. It originally sported four stories crowned by a high parapet at its roof, but that top floor disappeared in 1953. Note its recessed storefronts seemingly announced by cast iron columns.

2326–28 Strand

On the corner, Nicholas Clayton designed the two impressive three-story bank buildings in 1895. Originally known as the Ball, Hutchings-Sealy Buildings, they were the first steel-framed construction west of the Mississippi. Neo-Renaissance in design, note the dramatic gray and pink granite against red sand-

Hutchings-Sealy Buildings

stone. Inside, you'll find the original iron staircase with slate steps that lead up to the atrium floor on the second level.

2325 Strand

Across the street, you'll see part of what once was the three-story Phoenix Building. Brian M. McDonnell, proprietor of the Palmetto house, a fancy restaurant and hotel founded in 1839 by "Monsieur Alphonse" Aulauier, built it in 1870. According to Galveston Historical Foundation records, its cast iron front was almost totally destroyed during the surprise hurricane of 1943 (due to World War II), reducing the building to one story.

▶ Cross 24th Street.

2410–12 Strand

The only original structure in this block is the 1898 James Fadden Building in the middle of the next block. Note its false half-story at its roofline which makes it seem taller than it is. Another Clayton design, it once housed his wholesale wine, liquor and cigar business.

123 25th Street

The Santa Fe Building dramatically punctuates The Strand at its western end. Once two separate buildings with the street running between, its center expansion, designed by railroad architect E. A. Harrison in 1932, closed the street and covered the entire Strand facing with an Art Deco façade. One of the original 1876 structures was built as the headquarters and passenger terminal of the locally owned and operated, the Gulf, Colorado & Santa Fe Railroad. The Atcheson, Topeka and Santa Fe bought that company in 1886 only to merge with the International and Great Northern during the 1890s. The first floor of the building housed the Railroad Museum, which got "Iked."

▶ ❹ Cross The Strand and turn left on 25th Street (aka Rosenberg), walking south.

206 Rosenberg

Designed in 1913 by Lewis Green and Joseph Finger of Houston, the Panama Hotel was named to honor the city's close proximity to the man-made Canal. The building originally provided lodging for early 20th-century business men traveling by rail; recently, it has been converted into lofts. Even though loft conversions began in the Strand/Mechanic Historic District during the 1980s, each new project improves the concept with more accommodations for its prospective buyers.

▶ ❺ Turn left at Ship Mechanic's Row, also known as Mechanic, walking east on the north side of the street.

2422–2428 Mechanic

Originally designed by Nathaniel W. Tobey, Jr., for George Seeligson, the 1874 Sergeant Building provided lodging to new immigrants to the United States as the Hotel Texas at the beginning of the 20th century. It also warehoused the L. & H. Blum Company as well as Western Paper and an automobile showroom. This large brick building's most recent reincarnation as an art gallery replaced the double doors on the northwest corner of Mechanic with large windows. On its 25th Street side, you'll find residential lofts, complete with indoor parking for owners.

2413 Mechanic Avenue

Across the street is the rather plain Hanretta Building, also built in 1874, which represented the wholesale manufacturing industries of downtown Galveston. In 1985, it was reborn through restoration as second-floor apartments with retail on its ground level.

2402 Mechanic Avenue

Dominating the block, the Clarke and Courts Building housed the largest lithography company in the Southwest, Mexico and Cuba. Known for its quality work, this printing company led the industry for over 100 years. Designed by Nicholas Clayton in 1890, this five-story plant printed the first newspaper after the 1900 Storm. Its chief bookkeeper was one of the casualties.

Although its headquarters moved to Houston in 1936, this five-story Galveston plant remained in operation until it finally closed in 1989. The old Clarke and Courts building was then renovated into residential loft-apartments in 1994.

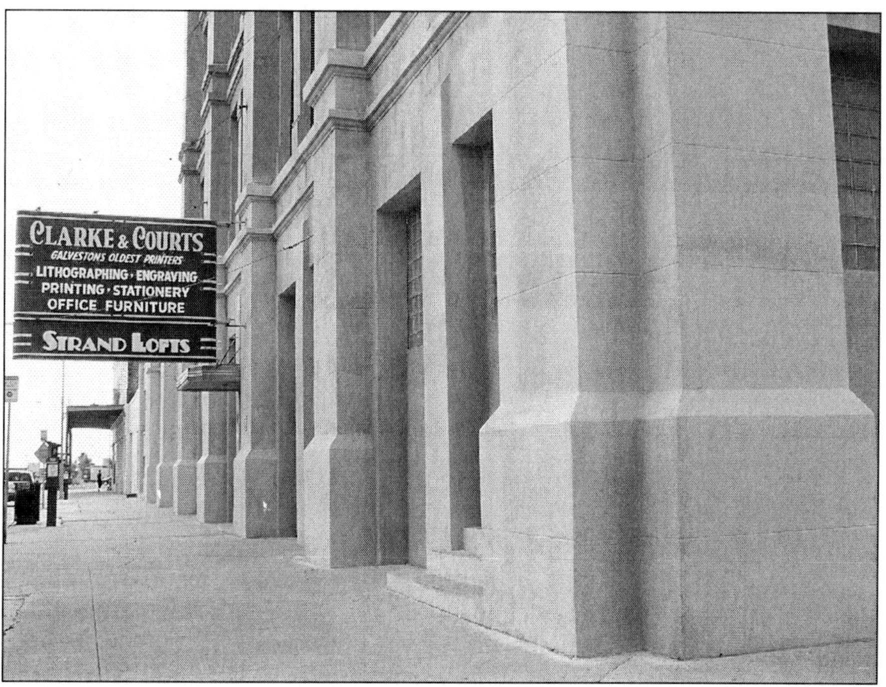

Clark and Courts Building

▶ Cross 24th Street.

2319–27 Mechanic Avenue

The catty-cornered Marx and Blum Building lost 3 of its 4 stories during the 1900 Storm. Even though Clayton had designed the original wholesale hat and shoe store in 1890, new owners Mistrot Brothers and Company hired C. W. Bulger to repair the damage in 1905, replacing only the second story for their ladies' clothing shop. The building received its present name from Jake and Harry Davidson who bought it in 1927 for their dry goods store. It became the Druss furniture warehouse in 1957 until it was transformed into the Davidson Ballroom of the Tremont House in 1995.

2300 Ship Mechanic's Row

Galveston's third Tremont House Hotel dominates the north side of the 2300 block of Mechanic Avenue. Two Alsatian Jewish brothers joined their cousin to establish the largest mercantile and wholesale dry goods business in Texas, housing its headquarters in the 1879 Leon & H. Blum Building. With offices nationwide and in Paris, the company expanded three years later only to dissolve in 1896 due to a national depression. They sold the building to the Mistrot brothers who closed their dry goods house in 1908. Then the *Galveston Tribune* moved in. In 1985, the Mitchells transformed the building into an elegant hotel. They celebrated its Grand Opening with the return of Galveston's Mardi Gras. Boone Powell's Arch was in place for the 1986 celebration. Since Leon Blum was once known as the "Merchant Prince of Texas," they named the restaurant in his honor. Of particular note is the rosewood Toujouse Bar in the Lobby, dating from the Opera House Saloon. Completing the Tremont House complex, the 1873 McDonnell Building on the corner, also known as the old Belmont Hotel, was incorporated in 1990. Note its cast iron street level façade. It is reported that a hotel has stood on this corner since 1841.

2309–17 Mechanic

Berlocher Row stands across the street. Built as investments by the Swiss commission merchant between 1858 and 1870, these three Greek Revival buildings once served the Confederate Army as a guardhouse. In 1876, John Berlocher defaulted on a loan from Gustave Opperman, whose heirs had lost the buildings to the Mistrot brothers. Their dry goods company kept their toy department here. Businesses such as Neiderman's Galveston Builders Supply came and went over the years. In 1979, the westernmost building became the Strand Street Theatre. All three were rehabilitated as the community theatre, offices, a bookstore and lofts by George and Cynthia Mitchell in 1993.

▶ **Cross 23rd Street.**

2222–2228 Mechanic

The old Washington Hotel once stood on this corner. Built in 1873 as the Cosmopolitan by the Welsh tin and coppersmith John Parker Davie, the building housed his Wholesale Builders Hardware on the first and fourth floors. Hotel rooms were on the second and third floors with the front desk and restaurant on the west side of the ground floor. Vacant since the 1970s, a fire during Hurricane Alicia in 1983 gutted it. Fortunately, architects had already completed drawings based of the hotel's exterior so, with the support of George and Cynthia Mitchell, they literally raised it from the ashes six years later.

2220 Mechanic

Another Davie structure stands on its east side, which pre-dates the original hotel by 18 years.

2214–16 Ship Mechanic's Row

John Sealy constructed the once-three story stuccoed brick building as an investment in 1873. During the 1960s, **2214** housed the Ching Wah Café.

2212 Mechanic Avenue

Left over from Galveston's wide-open gambling days, a casino teller's cage awaits a bet on this building's second floor—reportedly.

2202–10 Mechanic Avenue

At the corner of 22nd Street, Czechoslovakian brothers John and Gustav Reymerhoffer built their commission house in 1877, which specialized in imported glass and porcelain ware. Unfortunately, the building's unusual triple-gabled roof and architectural detail has been stripped over the years.

306 22nd Street.

Diagonally across the street once stood the impressive Grand Southern Hotel, which burned during the June 1877 fire. The present building replaced it the following year. Although built as an investment by merchant Samson Heidenheimer, it is best known by the name of his tenant, the H. Mosle Steamship agents. They established the first direct route between Galveston and South America.

▶ **Cross 22nd Street.**

220 22nd Street

You cannot help but notice the imposing 1882 Victorian/Italian Renaissance Kauffman & Runge Building that stands on the opposite corner. Once the "largest cotton exporting house" as agents for North German Lloyds, the firm went bankrupt in 1887 after Runge unsuccessfully attempted to corner the cotton market three years earlier. The building passed to the cotton and wool factor, Gustave Heye. After the 1900 Storm, Maco Stewart Sr. opened his new title company in this building after C. W. Bulger remodeled the original Eugene Heiner design.

212 22nd Street

Looking toward The Strand, note the 1882 H. M. Trueheart & Company Building on the alley. Nicholas Clayton incorporated

From left: First National Bank, H. M. Trueheart & Company Building, Stewart Title Company

the eclectic styles of Victorian, Corinthian, Greek and Romanesque in its multicolored brick and tile pattern to house the oldest real estate company west of the Mississippi. The Junior League restored it in 1971.

▶Continue walking east on Ship Mechanic's Row, back to your car.

2108 Mechanic Avenue

The complex Romanesque façade of the *Galveston Daily News* Building marks one of the best of Nicholas Clayton's early works. Note the red pressed brick accented with pink marble and terra cotta. Built as the first building in Texas dedicated solely to newspaper production, it cost $30,000 in 1884. After the *Daily News* moved out west on the Causeway in 1966, its ornate façade was covered with plaster panels which protected it for restoration in 1995.

Galveston Daily News Building

305 21st Street

The last 19th century office building you'll pass on your Strand/Mechanic Strut is the Heidenheimer Marine Building at the corner of 21st Street and Ship Mechanic's Row. Victorian Gothic in style with late medieval influences in its parapets and arches, this 1875 design housed Sampson Heidenheimer's lighterage company, which partially unloaded ships while in the Gulf so they could clear the sandbar at the mouth of the harbor. An immigrant from

Wurttemberg in 1858, he ran the Union blockades during the Civil War to establish his various other businesses, which included a salt warehouse, candy factory and bank until his death in 1891.

Heidenheimer Marine Building

▶Back at your car, this concludes your walk of Galveston's historic central business district, The Strand and Ship Mechanic's Row.

CHAPTER 2

East End Historical District

Due to Galveston's port, "a lotta people made a lotta money" from the 1840s through 1900. Successful Strand merchants built their homes in an adjacent residential area before the Civil War. Unfortunately, most of those early homes were lost in the Great Fire of November 1885.

Appropriately on a Friday the 13th, a fire left blazing in the Vulcan Ironworks furnace ignited neighboring houses while the city slept. A fierce north wind quickly spread the flames block by block from 16th and The Strand over 40 blocks, reducing 500 homes to ashes by daybreak and leaving 2,500 homeless. With the damage estimated at upwards of $2,000,000, a relief committee collected contributions of $55,000 that next day, including one from New York railroad magnate Jay Gould.

Within a week, a building boom ensued in the "Fire District" that continued the next ten years. Giving rise to a unique Galveston architectural style, it defined the decadent Gilded Age of the Gay '90s on Galveston Island.

One basic style—usually a form of Greek Revival—was modified to fit Island climate and lifestyle. High ceilings increased air circulation, as did cupolas and wrap-around porches with walk-through windows to combat the summer's heat. To accommodate the frequent "overflows" of this sea-level barrier island, homes were built 3–10 feet off the ground on brick piers. Elements of Italianate, Queen Ann, Colonial, Gothic and Classic Revivals, Romanesque to the later Craftsmen style melded into a general Victorian eclectic—truly "Galveston Style." Intermingled with this elegance were simple shotgun and tenant cottages, large boarding houses, even a castle.

Miraculously, this district was spared the wrath of the 1900 Storm. The wreckage of wood debris from the beachfront formed a breakwater on Broadway some thirty feet high and three miles long that protected the heart of the city.

With its preponderance of 19th century houses still standing, the Galveston City Council created the East End Historical District in 1971. By 1975, this 52-block area was listed in the National Register of Historic Places, and, one year later, officially recognized as a national historic landmark district by the Texas Historical Commission—the first on Galveston Island. As you leisurely walk its tree-lined streets, many deemed impassable for large motor coaches, pay close attention to the details of design within each home—from the many varieties of gingerbread and verandas, dramatic turrets, innovative surfaces, stained-glass windows and wrought-iron fences.

Due to the size of the District—a full 1,500 acres—you'll explore it in two walks: West Side Wandering and the East Side Stories, bordering the Medical Branch. Both begin and end in areas of popular eateries on Postoffice, the first at 21st Street and the second on 14th Street.

Enjoy your architectural exploration of Galveston's East End.

West Side Wandering

▶ ❶ Park your car on 20th Street, between Postoffice and Church avenues. Since you'll have to "plug" a parking meter, have lunch either before or after your walk, and leave your car in the restaurant's parking lot.

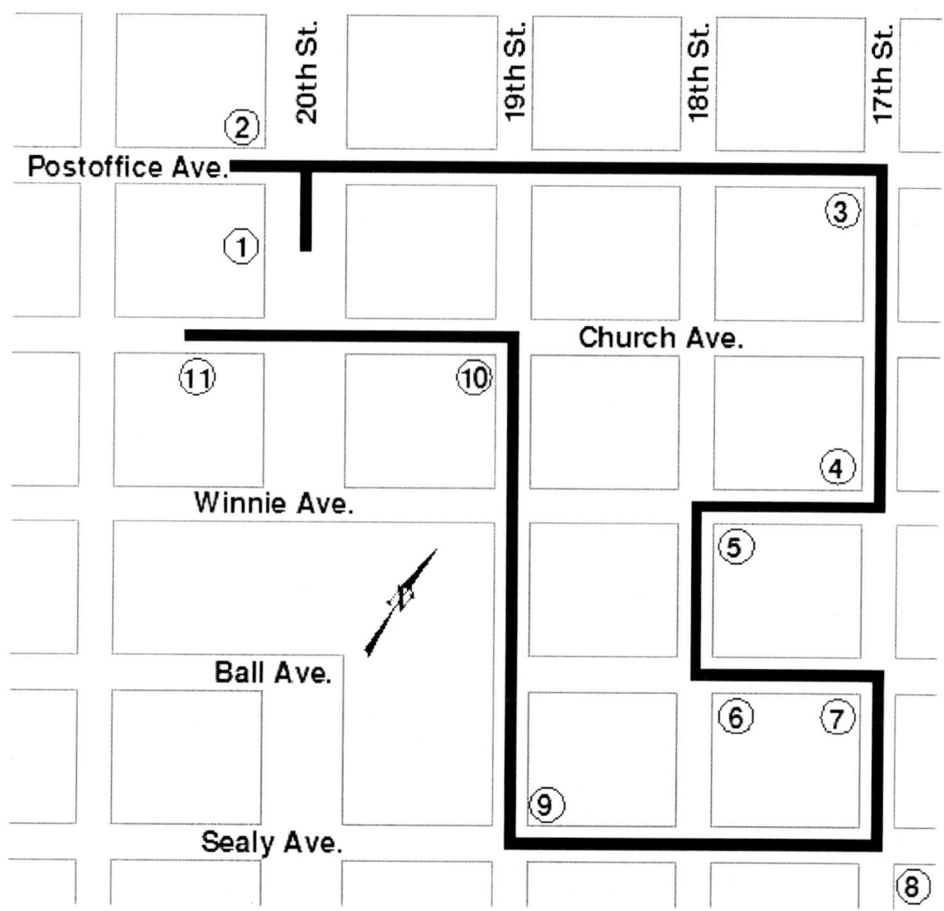

2012–20 Postoffice Avenue

Continue your journey into Galveston's past at the Grand 1894 Opera House, marked by its Romanesque carved stone arch. For a closer look, you'll find it one-half block to the left. The *Galveston Daily News* proclaimed the theatre "the grandest temple to Thespis in . . . the Southwest" the day after it opened on January 3, 1895. Architect Frank Cox of New Orleans employed many innovative techniques in his theatrical design, producing a house with no square corners and curved proscenium arch which created marvelous acoustics. This feature saved the Grand from the wrecking ball. Its complete restoration in 1986 transformed the Opera House into an intimate but modern, fully functioning performing arts hall without compromising the integrity of its original design. Although the only outward sign of its grandeur is its arch, a self-guided tour is encouraged and certainly worth the nominal charge.

The Grand 1894 Opera House before the 1900 Storm
—Courtesy of The Rosenberg Library, Galveston, Texas

▶ ❷ Turn to the right, retracing your steps to the corner, and continue walking east.

1927 Postoffice Avenue

At the southeast corner of 20th Street stands the Old Federal

Building, marked by its columns. Built in a record 114 days in 1861 so the contractor would get paid before the South seceded from the Union, this classic Greek Revival sports Ionic columns on its first floor with Corinthian columns on the second. It now houses the administrative offices of the Galveston Historical Foundation.

1907 Postoffice Avenue

Next door was the Bertha Wieting House. Behind that facing 19th Street at **507**, another built in 1886 by the widow of a successful real estate agent, Eliza Moser. Both of these houses burned on September 12 even before Hurricane Ike came ashore, as firefighters were kept away by the already-high water.

▶Cross 19th St., walking east on the north side of Postoffice Avenue

Beginning your first journey into the residential East End, this street serves as the historic district's western border south to Broadway. Most of the homes in the next two blocks of Postoffice were built immediately after the Great Fire of 1885. Abraham Cohen, manager of Leon & H. Blum dry goods, built the interesting duplex at **1818** in 1886.

1816 Postoffice Avenue

That same year, Theodore Ohmstede built this home for his family next door. This Galveston-style Victorian home features two-story front porches, architecturally referred to as "double galleries," with walk-through windows, so typical of time and place, for maximum cooling. Next door, the small 1950s ivy-covered building once housed a beauty shop. However, the small shop, pictured on the next page, is no longer standing.

1808 and 1802 Postoffice Avenue

The next two Queen Anne designs were the handiwork of German architect, Alfred Muller who was known for his use of fancy wood trim and millwork, or ornate gingerbread. Built for prosperous grocer Alfred Rakel in 1887, note how these twins telescope back to the carriage house, not only to capture the breezes but also to enlarge the view.

Muller Twins

1801 Postoffice

The building directly across the street was originally built as a boarding house in 1887 but became the playhouse of the Little Theatre of Galveston in 1926.

1724 Postoffice

In this block, a concrete embankment, or parapet, connects the houses on the north side of the street, beginning with this rather simple high raised townhouse. Note its gingerbread, a standout with contrasting paint. To capture the cool southern breezes, the north side of the street was preferred. Most of the houses on the south side of any street throughout the city are much plainer than those facing them.

1720 Postoffice Avenue

Nicholas Clayton, Galveston's foremost architect and master builder, designed this home for surgeon Dr. Arthur Sampson in 1889. Its wrap-around, curved galleries features Stick style in the pattern of its gingerbread to showcase the off-center double front door and gabled roof. The house served as rental property from 1903 until it was restored in 1989.

1710 Postoffice Avenue

Note the next two Victorians, noteworthy for their wrap-around porches. Real estate broker William Reppen built the second in 1889. It features a unique rounded bay as well as fish-scale siding so common throughout the East End.

1717 Postoffice Avenue

On the south side of the street, this gabled house was built for Mrs. Elise C. Michael in 1890.

1702 Postoffice Avenue

Still connected by the parapet but deviate from the wood-framed houses is this 1905 design by George B. Stowe on the corner. Built by British-born insurance man John D. Hodson, this large stucco-covered brick house combines Colonial Revival with Craftsman Style, signaling this transitional period. Its unassuming façade belies its rich interior of mahogany, oak inlaid floors and beautiful stained glass, as seen in the entry doors and transom which feature a unique oleander motif. The house is now a Bed and Breakfast.

1628 Postoffice

Nicholas Clayton designed this Southern townhouse on this northeast corner. Built by restaurateur Rudolph Kruger in the spring of 1889, its 17th Street side features a second entrance, a servants' porch shaded by wooden louvered blinds. The present owners have chosen not to paint its cypress exterior.

▶ ❸ Turn right. Cross Postoffice, walking south on 17th Street.

511 17th Street

The massive Issac Heffron Home houses Galveston's oldest Bed and Breakfast. Designed by Charles W. Bulger in 1899 for the Welsh concrete contractor this house was constructed completely of cement, covered with a red brick veneer. From a distance, its color and wide wrap-around veranda suggest a steamboat. Legend has it that the spirits of both Mr. and Mrs. are still in residence.

615 17th Street

On the west side of the street, this later-built house is unique for its steep gabled roof and dormer window.

▶ Cross Church Avenue

1627 Church

Saloon proprietor Edward A. Colleraine built this Clayton Southern townhouse in 1908 as well as the house behind it at **612 17th Street**. Note the second entry, seemingly leading to a separate apartment.

1701 Church

Wholesale grocer Ernest Stavenhaven built this tenant home in May 1922.

1702 and 1706 Church

Mrs. Maude Moller built both of these homes as tenant houses in 1895. One of the first women real estate developers on the Island, she and her husband, Jens, moved from their Sealy Avenue home into another of her rentals at **513 17th Street** after his retirement in 1902. Apparently rental properties made good investments during this time.

▶ 4 Turn right on Winnie Avenue

1702 Winnie Avenue

Charles Vidor from Hungary built this home for his family in 1886. His son, King, who was literally born and raised here, went on to achieve Hollywood success during The Depression as a celebrated movie producer/director. In 1938, he directed the black-&-white episodes of *The Wizard of Oz* for his friend, David Selznick, who was busy with his epic, *Gone with the Wind*. The cottage next door belonged to A. Wilkins Miller, who was president of the Miller and Vidor Lumber Company.

King Vidor was born and raised in this house.

1701 Winnie

On the south side of the street, H. J. Hagleman's asymmetrical raised Victorian cottage contrasts Vidor's home. Note its double curved roofs over the porch. On both sides of the street, this block of Winnie offers a variety of Victorian residences.

1707 Winnie

Built by Galvestonian R. B. Garret, the cottage next door also belonged to A. Wilkins Miller.

1709-1711 Winnie

Built in 1888 as rental homes for J. P. Davie, these two narrow houses feature peaked gables and covered verandas.

1712 Winnie

The stately Victorian across the street was built in 1886 for Yetta Heidenheimer and Abraham Davis. Centered above the double galleries, you'll see a medallion within its gable. This contrasts with the off-centered entry door to the left.

1719 Winnie

Stevedore Louis Zimmerman's home replaced another destroyed in the 1885 fire.

1722 and 1724 Winnie

Of particular interest are these classic twin shotgun tenant cottages built by Charles A. Harris. The name of this Southern style comes from the implication that one could fire a shotgun through the front door and out the back door without hitting any interior walls.

1727 Winnie

The house on the south corner was built as a tenant home in 1893 by real estate agent Asbury Casteel. When contrasted with the next block of restored houses, these homes are obviously awaiting rebirth by restoration but at least they are still standing.

▶ 5 Turn left on 18th Street, walking south to Ball Avenue

1801 Ball Avenue

On the southwest corner, meat supplier Alfred Newson's 1896 rather plain raised two-story house paid homage to Clayton's 1887 grander design for Louis Block across the street. This was demolished in the late 1960s to make way for apartments. Haunting occurrences have been reported here.

▶ 6 Cross Ball Avenue and turn left, walking east on the south side of the street.

1724 Ball Avenue

Carpenter James H. Kissinger built a high-raised two-story with an unusual single veranda in 1901.

1721, 1715, 1711 and 1709 Ball

Mrs. Dorothea Juneman's four rent houses dominate the south side of this block. While Mrs. Moller built larger homes throughout the district, this carpenter's widow invested in small cottages after the Great Fire of 1885. She built her first at **1715** in 1886 and her last next door eight years later. Richard Coon's 1893 Southern townhouses built in 1892 at **1719**, contrasts with Juneman's quaint tenant cottages. Note how they have been made picturesque by contemporary paint patterns to accent their fish scale siding. Larger Painted Ladies decorate three corners of 17th and Ball.

1712 Ball Avenue

Built in 1888 for W. C. Ogelivy, the superintendent of the Southern Cotton Press, this home features a double gallery with an decorative frieze above.

1702 Ball Avenue

Cotton clerk Frederick Beissner built this ornate home in 1886. Designed by William Roystone, the distinctive sunflower motif within its abundant gingerbread was perhaps prompted by playwright Oscar Wilde who had spoken of the "decorative art" in Galveston four years earlier. Hiding a widow's walk on the roof, this Queen Anne features a catty-cornered entrance,

The Beissner House

which the plain house across 17th Street tried to replicate in 1899.

1701 Ball

Note the high gables of the 1887 Norton/Waamoth home on the south corner.

▶ 7 Turn right on 17th Street and walk one block south to Sealy Avenue

1627 Sealy Avenue

At the corner of 17th and Sealy stands the "strangest house . . . in a city of strange houses": the Trube Castle. Originally a gardener in Denmark, John C. Trube made his fortune in Houston Real Estate. In 1890, he hired German architect Alfred Muller to build his dream house. It's thought that the knavish Trube sought to "thumb his nose" at the conservative Island elite. Based on his memories of a castle in Keil, this raised house is complete with a mock tower. This house is actually brick, covered with a rusticated finish: a mixture of crushed oyster shells, concrete and water

The Trube Castle

which is then sculpted to appear as cut stone. Cross 17th Street for a closer look.

▶ 8 Turn right on Sealy Avenue, walking west on the north side of the street.

The canopy of trees over Sealy Avenue shades the homes in the next two blocks. These were among the first to be privately restored during Galveston's architectural renaissance of the 1970s, and much has been researched and written about them.

1702 Sealy

Catty-cornered from the castle is a Queen Anne rental house built in 1909 by Mrs. Sophia Hansen. Its neighbor was built five years earlier. Both stand across the street from the walled garden of the League home at 1710 Broadway.

1716 Sealy Avenue

This imposing home, perhaps unfairly upstaged by both corner houses, was built by harbor pilot, J. B. Woolford in 1896. A. L. Pierson, who owned the first company in Texas to use machines to produce clothing, bought the house in 1913. Note its substantial front door.

1728 Sealy Avenue

Charles Clarke, owner of a marine construction and dredging company, started construction on this corner house in 1899. Designed by George Stowe, it sits on an arched basement with expansive bays, gabled roof and a turret to lend it an air of grandeur despite its rusticated veneer. Legend had it that Clarke had many daughters to marry off, because its grand mahogany staircase, rising perpendicular to the entry, contains a small step-up balcony called a bridal bow. This house sold as "not complete" in 1928 to grain exporter and foreign Consul, Julius W. Jockusch. It was his daughter, Hedda, who tossed her bouquet from the bridal bow during the 1930s. A carriage house stands to the east of the home. A decorated World War I seaman, Charles Clarke died on October 20, 1940, at his home on Avenue Q ½.

1727 Sealy Avenue

A blue and white Queen Ann/Eastlake design fills the opposite corner. Having achieved his fortune in shipping, Samuel Maas returned to Germany in 1844 to propose marriage to Isabella Offenback, sister of French composer Jacques. He built her this home in 1887.

▶ **Cross 18th Street.**

1802 Sealy Avenue

The Maas' son, Max, proudly served as State and County Tax Collector, and incorporated the Texas star above the windows of his Southern townhouse built in 1886.

1814 Sealy Avenue

Next to the 1890 home of Mrs. Abraham Levy, this 1886 Southern townhouse was originally built for dry goods merchant, Jacob S. Bernheim. Danish ship broker Jens Moller bought it during the 1890s, while his wife Maude built rental houses. George B. Stowe designed the house next door in 1897 as rental property. This Victorian features a corner turret on its west side with a bay window to the east.

1815 Sealy

On the south side of the block, this simple George B. Stowe design was built in 1898 for Joseph Goldstein and his two sisters.

1817 Sealy

In sharp contrast stands the elaborate gingerbread of the 1907 Wansker house next door, which sold to Adolph and Catherine Dolson in 1937. It earned a marker from the Texas Historical Commission because Dolson served as the city's Finance Director from 1943 until his death in 1950.

1819 Sealy

Insurance records report this home was built from salvaged debris from the 1900 Storm.

1826 Sealy Avenue

The epitome of Victoriana on Galveston Island can clearly be seen at the corner of 19th and Sealy. Built by wholesale dry goods and insurance agent Jacob Sonnentheil in 1888, its architectural style fuses elements of Eastlake with Greek Revival, French Second Empire and Italianate to create "Carpenter Gothic." It is thought that Nicholas Clayton designed the house, although no solid evidence exists. After Sonnentheil went bankrupt, Charles J. Stubbs bought the vacant house in 1911. When first restored in 1977, the house served as a law office; now it is a single-family dwelling, complete with carriage house.

Jacob Sonnentheil built this Carpenter Gothic in 1888.

▶ 9 Turn right to walk north on 19th Street.

812 19th Street and 1827 Ball Avenue

You'll pass two high-raised tenant houses, also built by Mrs.

Moller, on one lot. The simpler first design on the alley bears a marker noting the year they were built: 1895. Next door, the elaborate Queen Anne with its curving stairway and turret belies its rental status. The Texas Historical Commission recognized the Mollers and their Swiss Consul tenant, Ulrich Muller, with a plaque in 1983. Looking down Ball Avenue, please note the uniform symmetry of the front porches on this block.

The Maud Moller rentals

▶ **Continue walking north on 19th Street.**

Newer construction dominates the east side of 19th Street, including a Greek Orthodox Church and an apartment complex. The west side is filled with county government buildings. Look east on Ball and Winnie avenues for more Victorian designs.

1903 Church

At the corner of 19th Street and Church Avenue, you'll find the

First Presbyterian Church. On January 1, 1840, the congregation was organized at this location by Rev. John McCullough—the first faith on Galveston Island. This building was the brain child of R. F. Bunting, known as the "Fighting Parson" of Terry's Texas Rangers during the Civil War. Construction started on January 23, 1873, when the cornerstone was laid and the chapel, which sits behind the sanctuary facing Church Street, started construction. Worship began here when it was completed in 1876. However, economic conditions slowed the church's progress. The Memphis, Tennessee, architectural firm of Jones and Baldwin sent 31-year-old Nicholas J. Clayton to Galveston to supervise the construction. In 1887, he added his own tower to Edward C. Jones' design. "Bunting's Folly" was finally consecrated in 1889, at a cost of $90,000, but First Presbyterian still stands today as the finest example of Norman architecture in the Southwest.

Clayton proved to be one of the city's best success stories. Born in Cork County, Ireland, on November 1, 1849, this master-builder-to-be immigrated to Cleveland, Ohio, at the age of two, with his widowed mother. In 1874 he established his own company in Galveston, designing and remodeling churches, commercial buildings and residences both on and off the Island until his death in 1916. The prolific "N.J."—so called by family and friends—created a monumental architectural legacy that still stands today in Galveston, and beyond. So great was his influence on the Island's ambiance, author Howard Barnstone called the last 25 years of the nineteenth century the "Clayton Era" in his *Galveston That Was*.

▶ ⑩ Turn left on Church Avenue, walking west to 21st Street.

2011 Church Avenue

The first church built on Galveston Island was St. Mary's Cathedral, located at the corner of 21st Street. The parish was established in 1841. Six of its original priests died ministering to the victims of the 1844 Yellow Fever epidemic. The family of one of them, Father Paquin, sent 500,000 bricks from Antwerp, Belgium, to build a memorial cathedral for the new Texas diocese. When this American Gothic Revival, designed by Theodore

E. Giraud, was completed in 1848, the closest cathedral was in Monterrey, Mexico. With 14 diocesan cathedrals in the state to its credit, Pope John Paul II declared St. Mary's a Minor Basilica in 1979 due to its historical significance.

After a hurricane destroyed the original central tower in 1876, Bishop Gallagher commissioned Clayton to design another to hold the 15 foot metal statue of St. Mary two years later. Legend has it that as long as the Blessed Mother, Star of the Sea, remains atop her tower, Galveston is safe. Indeed, it was the bells of St. Mary's that brought much solace and hope to 1900 Storm survivors that devastating Sunday in September.

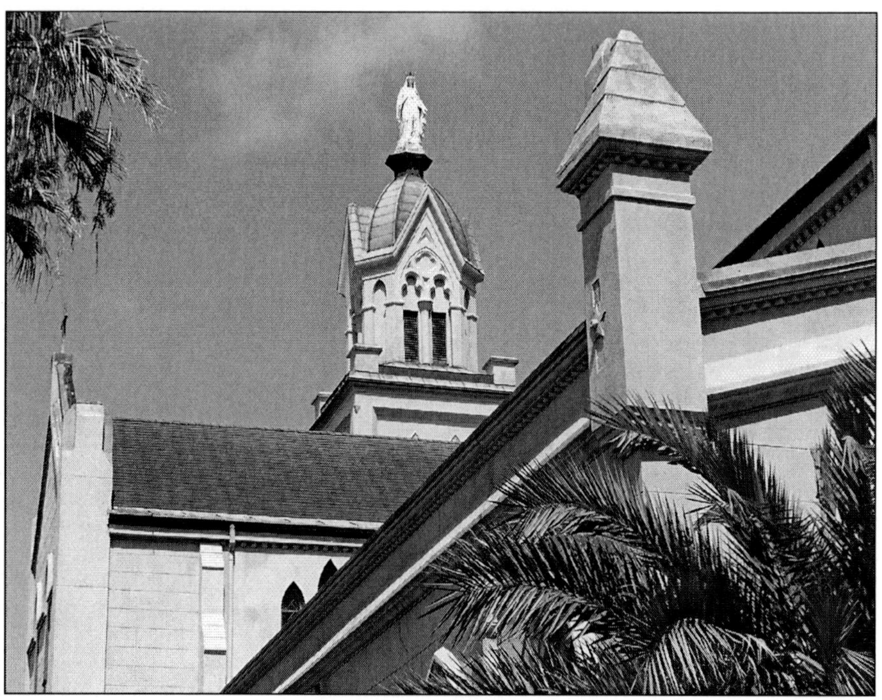

St. Mary's Cathedral

▶ ⑪ Retrace your steps east to 20th Street, where your car is parked—unless you parked in a restaurant's parking lot. This concludes your first walk of Galveston's historic residential East End Historical District.

East Side Stories

▶ ❶ Park your car at 13th and Postoffice Avenue.

1302 Postoffice

You'll find yourself in front of the 1886 Gus Reymershoffer Home. With the profits from their Texas Star Flour Mill, which was located at Harborside and 22nd Streets, both he and his brother could well afford to build their dream homes. Older brother John built the larger of the two on the corner of 14th

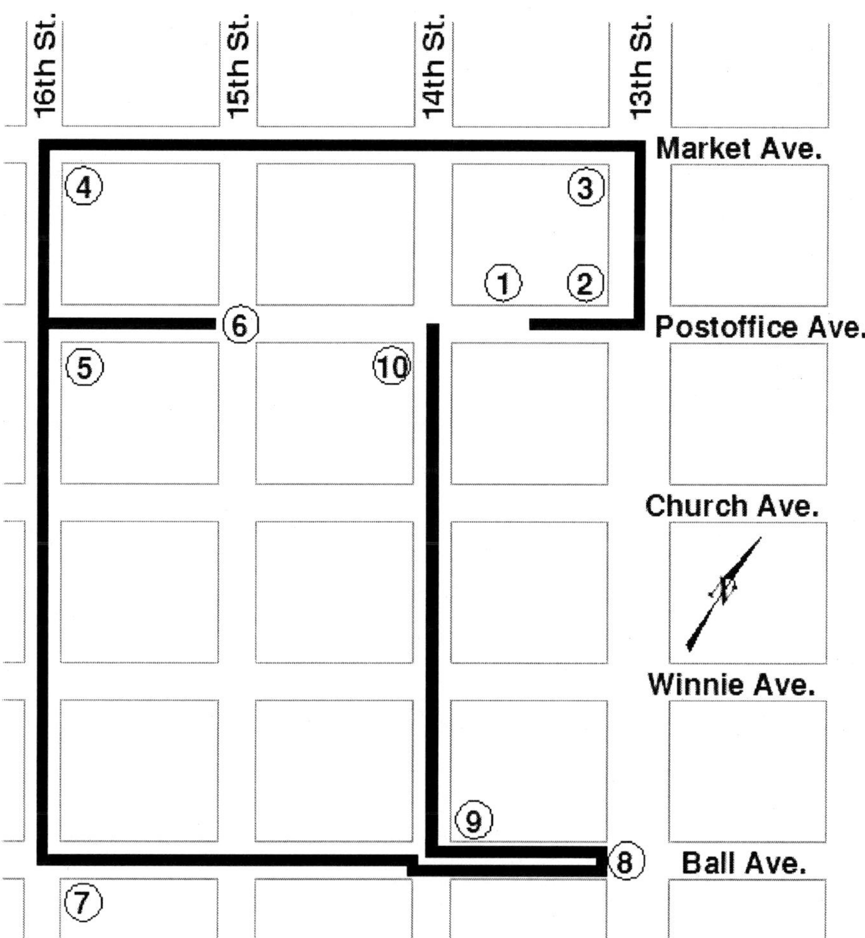

Street and Postoffice. Featuring a tower room, balcony and conservatory, it housed the Phi Chi medical fraternity from 1925 until it was demolished in December 1956. Next door, Gus' Victorian Eclectic "cottage" maintains the original checkered sidewalk and cast iron fence, which still bears the name, "G. Reymershoffer" on the gate. Although of Austrian birth, the Reymershoffers were considered German since they chose to live in this area of Galveston's Germanic elite.

416 13th Street

Across 13th Street stands the dilapidated home of Gustav Heye, who interceded with Mexico during the Civil War to ensure cotton shipments through the Port of Galveston. Built in 1880, this Victorian villa features a fish-scale shingled tower with a candle-snuffer roof at the corner of its south-facing veranda.

▶ ❷ Turn left and walk north to Market Avenue on the west side of 13th Street.

1301 Market

Across the alley from the Reymershoffer's house, merchant Louis H. Runge built this villa home in 1916. Architect Anton F. Korn, representing the New York firm of Crow, Lewis and Wickenhoefer, faced its Tuscan entry on 13th Street, even though its address should face Market Street. Miss Elisabeth D. Runge, librarian at the medical school from 1922 to 1968, sold it to UTMB. It served as the president's home after restoration in 1989. Recently, it's been sold again, with the profit going toward medical research and healthcare for the indigent.

▶ ❸ Turn left on Market Avenue. Look across the street.

1306 Market

The 1859 Henry Rosenberg home dominates this corner. Built by the Swiss immigrant destined to become Galveston's largest benefactor, this Italianate Villa reflected its owner's wealth with understated Southern elegance. Many of the materials were imported from Switzerland. Its exterior design features a balcony over its single-story veranda and a rooftop cupola. Inside the home, you'll find eight marble fireplaces, a hand carved plaster ceiling and tall wall mirrors but, unfortunately, the house is rarely opened to the public. In 1990, the Sealy Smith Foundation bought and restored it to serve as a conference and guest home for the University of Texas Medical Branch.

Deep within the campus you'll find the first medical school in the state. As business flourished and the city grew, Galveston's population was decimated at regular intervals by Yellow Fever. To discover its cause, a medical community gathered on the Island, lead by Connecticut-born and Yale graduate, Dr. Asbel Smith, who wrote the first treatise in Texas on the subject in 1839. A gifted speaker and diplomat, Smith used power and politics to establish the Texas Medical College in 1873. Its first structure was named in his honor even though he died five years before its construction. Designed by Nicholas Joseph Clayton in 1890, the Romanesque Revival building

The 1859 Henry Rosenberg home
—Courtesy of the University of Texas Medical Branch

boasts masonry of Texas sandstone, red pressed brick and granite. Because of its striking color, the Asbel Smith Building is affectionately nicknamed "Old Red." When it was slated for demolition in UTMB's Master Plan of 1965, it was allowed to deteriorate. Its once grand east wing, the original anatomy amphitheater, became home to pigeons—living, dead and dying. Alumni, faculty and the Galveston Historical Foundation succeeded in saving "Old Red" in 1983; its restoration was completed three years later.

Awaiting rebirth by restoration, the homes that border the UTMB campus were built circa 1868–1877. However, the next block of Market embraces several that have been restored, on both sides of the street.

▶ **Cross 14th Street on the south side of the street.**

1409 Market Avenue

The asymmetrical W. F. Breath Home is an "elaborate two-story house," built in 1886. As evidenced by the pattern of its gingerbread, it is one of the few Victorian Stick houses on the Island. Breath formed a partnership with Sam Houston's nephew, Sam Penland, as auctioneers and wholesale boot and shoe suppliers. He sold the home in 1895 to William Parr, owner of a steamship company that operated between Galveston and England. Dr. William Keiller acquired the house in 1922. Born in Scotland and educated at the Edinburgh University, he was the leading American anatomist for forty years and the first professor of anatomy at the University of Texas Medical Branch.

1412 Market Avenue

Across the avenue, Nicholas Clayton designed the raised two-story home for insurance agent and public school board trustee, Isadore Lovenberg. Built in 1877, this large Southern townhouse features a vertical orientation. Note the central peaked roof upper porch trimmed in detailed gingerbread. The sprawling Sam Levy House next door at **1414 Market** struggles to copy these features.

1417 Market Avenue

With its clapboard-covered double front porch, the 1893 John Hanna home is perhaps the most distinctive house on this side of the street. A real estate agent and amateur photographer, Hanna's interior images, taken in this house, documented the household of a Galveston middle-income family during the 1890s.

1426 Market Avenue

The 1885 Peter Gengler Home proudly stands on the corner. This classic Greek Revival with its central hall was designed in 1885 by Galveston's foremost architect and master builder, Nicholas Clayton, for the German grocer and his family. Note the gingerbread on its gabled entryway. The bay window on its east side once overlooked a substantial garden, which gave way to a newer house in 1956. Clayton also designed his retail grocery store at 2009-13 Market in 1893, which is not longer standing.

▶ **Cross both Market Avenue and 15th Street.**

1502 Market Avenue

The white plantation-style home across 15th Street was built in 1851 by Lorenzo Sherwood. He sold it to Edward T. Austin, cousin to Stephen F. Austin, the "Father of Texas," in 1870. Set

Edward Austin's white plantation-style home

amidst tall live oaks, this Greek Revival with Gothic Revival influences features a rambling wrap-around veranda, designed to maximize southern breezes. Note the louvered blinds on the servants' wing and carriage house on the west side of the property. Lawyer Austin held several public offices, including mayor and county judge.

1520 Market

Next door, the brick 1859 Greek Revival home of grocer George W. Grover stands behind its vintage iron fence. Without shutters, it appears rather plain. The next two houses were built as rental houses in 1913 by jeweler M. W. Shaw.

▶ ④ Turn left on 16th St., staying on the east side of the street. You'll be walking south.

Twenty Dominican sisters arrived on Galveston Island September 19, 1882, at the request of Bishop Gallagher of St. Mary's Cathedral. They established the Sacred Heart Academy the following month at 14th and Broadway. After that church was destroyed during the 1900 Storm, the school was moved here to the 1882 Bertrand Adoue House, another Clayton design. In 1927, the name was changed to Dominican High School, which became a girls-only Catholic school in 1940 with a new building. The Adoue house was torn down to make way for a new convent in 1953. Both were designed by Raymond Rapp. The high school closed in 1968.

1602 Postoffice Avenue

On the alley across 16th Street, note the two-story stable and servants' quarters which served the big red brick house on the corner.

Wholesale grocer and cotton factor, Henry A. Landes built the fortress-like, brooding Romanesque house in 1886. A veteran of the Battle of Galveston on the Confederate side, he hired George E. Dickey to design his family's home. With his resources as a partner in one of the city's largest mercantile firms, Landes imported many of its building materials. Even though much of the elaborate trim on the original Mansard roof was lost in the 1900 Storm, the three-story turret survived. John P. McDonough, owner of an Iron Works company, admired its Queen Anne cast ironwork and bought it in 1911; hence, the Landes-McDonough Home. Fifty years later, his heirs gave it to the Dominican Sisters, who ran the Catholic girls' school. The house is now being restored as a single-family dwelling.

▶5 Cross Postoffice Avenue. Turn left and walk one block east, walking on the south side of the street.

The north side of this block, formerly Dominican, now serves as the Transitional Learning Center for head-injured patients.

1527 Postoffice Avenue

Wholesale merchant Ernest Stavenhagen built the two-story Neo-classical home in 1913, at the age of 70. He came to Galveston after the Civil War, having served in DeBray's Confederate regiment. His company, Ernest Slavenhagen and Son, was a commission house specializing in produce and poultry. Note his house's impressive entry portico, with its double gallery and boxed classical colonnade. His heirs sold the house in 1948 to pharmacist Edmund J. Cordray, who used it as rental property. Cordray built the Craftsman and Colonial Revival next door at **1521** in 1914, leasing it to the Alpha Kappa Kappa medical fraternity until his daughter Florence Beaulieu—also a pharmacist—moved in with her family in 1941, staying until 1985. Note its Doric columns.

1509 Postoffice Avenue

Welsh native Isaac Heffron was just two years old when his family moved to Galveston Island in 1860. Growing up with the frontier port and its various epidemics, concrete contractor Heffron proposed both the city's first sewer system, which was approved by the City Council in 1886, and the Galveston Water Works, which was established in 1889. One year later, he and his wife, Clotilde, built this ten room home, which is still distinguished by its concrete and iron fence along the sidewalk. Ten years later, they moved up and into to the sprawling red brick villa at 511 17th Street, which is on the "West Side

Wanderings." Their daughter, Clotilde and husband, Andrew Faligant, lived here briefly after they returned from Europe. Pharmacist Edmund J. Cordray bought the Heffron house from Galveston's state senator Thomas Jefferson Holbrook in 1940. The south side of this block of Postoffice became somewhat of a Cordray family enclave, with his house, his daughter and son-in-law next door, and mother-in-law Mrs. Beaulieu at **1515**.

1501–03 Postoffice Avenue

In 1918, Cordray moved his drug store to the corner of 15th and Postoffice, which was reportedly built on Galveston's original slave block. In 1967, the Texas State Historical Survey Committee designated it a Historic Landmark because John S. Sydnor, one of the city's earliest mayors, operated slave auctions on the site. Somehow, that TSHSC plate has disappeared over the years. The drugstore was demolished in the early 1970s and the Victor Gustafson cottage was moved here in 1979 to serve as the headquarters of the East End Historic District Association.

▶ ❻ Retrace your steps on picturesque Postoffice, crossing 16th Street to the west side of the street.

1601 Postoffice Avenue

Thomas E. Bollinger, a clerk for the W. H. Simpson grocery and feed store appropriately located on Market, built his "cottage" in 1906. He and his wife, Maggie, lived here with their daughter, Miss Stella, who was a teacher at Rosenberg School in 1925. Nurse Alice Angie Mullen bought the house in 1948 after it had served as rental property, and lived here until her death in 1987. Located on the southwest corner, note the wraparound porch of this simplified Queen Anne. Directly behind at **509 16th Street** stands another Bollinger home with its original stained glass windows still intact.

▶ Continue walking south on the west side of the street.

Little is known about many of the houses in the next two blocks of 16th Street, as chances are they've never been restored or researched. Think of the potential!

1602 Church Avenue

One of the oldest houses in the East End Historical District was built by pioneer Texas newspaperman Wilbur Cherry. Born in New York in 1820, he fought in the Texas Revolution before coming to Galveston to found the *Galveston Weekly News* on January 6, 1844. He built this simple Greek Revival home in 1852. Miraculously, it escaped the flames of the 1885 fire. At the time of his death in 1873, he was working as a printer for the newspaper he had founded.

1607 Church

Across the street, note the abundant gingerbread, especially the fish scale siding and spindles of this cute raised cottage, built in 1903 by F. H. Sage, manager of Texas Transport.

**Cross Church Avenue**

1527 Church Avenue

Featured on the cover of September 19, 1999, *Texas* magazine within the *Houston Chronicle*, this two-story corner grocery store/home is typical of the corner stores scattered throughout the city. The Texas Superette, owned by Sebastiano and Angelina Tropea, featured a corner entrance and sidewalk canopy. So common throughout the city, they inspired their own book—*The Corner Store: An American Tradition, Galveston Style* by Ellen Beasley. Please notice that two corner grocery stores are only a block apart on 16th Street.

1602 Winnie

German grocer Senechal built this house in 1901 as both house and business. The family sold the cube-shaped store to the Novelli family in 1922, who continued to operate it until 1939. Their son, Ross, was born above the store.

▶ **Cross Winnie Avenue.**

1601 Winnie

According to insurance records, this home was built in 1892 by

H. Bankfield, while the raised cottage next door was built circa 1890.

714 16th Street

Mid-block on the east side, A. M. Hampton built this home in 1912. Sometime during its lifetime, it housed apartments. Some have asserted that the corner house next door was built in 1842. However, photographs show that this block was leveled during the 1900 Storm, so it was probably more like 1914.

1602 Ball Avenue

The impressive Painted Lady of Joel B. Wolfe stands at the corner of 16th and Ball. The heavy machinery salesman built the home in 1886 to replace another which was consumed in the 1885 fire. This impressive Queen Anne was once known as "Maison des Fleurs" for the floral patterns within the gingerbread. Because of the similarities of their decorative woodwork, some speculate that it was also designed by William Roystone, architect of the Frederick W. Beissner house at the corner of 17th and Ball. Note the Widow's Walk from across the street.

▶ **Cross Ball Avenue.**

1601 Ball Avenue

Even though its address is on Ball Avenue, the front porch of the unique 1887 Howard L. Mather Home, with its original double Dutch front doors, faces 16th Street. For easier access, the current owners have gated both streets as entries. Under a sloping roof, the unique

1887 Howard L. Mather Home

house combines elements of Queen Anne and Swiss Chalet to create a singular architectural style: High Victorian Chalet. Inside, amber stained glass over the bay windows of the Library and stairway create sunny warmth to the entry of this Bed and Breakfast, even when no fire is in the fireplace.

▶ ❼ Turn left on Ball, walking east.

802 16th Street

Directly across the street from the Mather Home, Nicholas Clayton remodeled an existing house, perhaps rental property, in 1892 for Mrs. George Ball and her son Frank.

1517 Ball

Next to a 1900 Storm Survivor stands "The Cottage." Built in 1882 for commission merchant Bernard Roensch, this unusual house features a central doorway with leaded Tiffany glass in its transoms, a gabled front porch and polygonal tower. Late Greek Revival with high Victorian detail, it is being restored, from the inside out. According to *Funk and Wagnall's New Practical Standard Dictionary of 1952*, Roensch earned his living by serving as an agent who bought and sold goods for others: a commission merchant.

1522 Ball Avenue

Look across the avenue to note the 1890 Southern townhouse built for James Findlay of Ball, Hutchings and Company.

1516 Ball Avenue

Built in 1897 and designed by Charles W. Bulger for insurance exec William F. Beers, this Queen Anne had a "face lift" twenty years later that changed its façade to craftsman style. Next door at **1512 Ball** stands the 1891 Walter F. Ayres house, perhaps the work of Alfred Muller.

1502 Ball Avenue

Note the W. B. Lockhart house on the northwest corner of Ball and 15th Street. Originally built as a one story Queen Anne cottage in 1889, a major renovation in 1905 raised it and added a new ground floor, with elements of Colonial Revival. After all, this admiralty lawyer and prominent court justice had married well—Walter Gresham's oldest daughter, Esther. Note the leaded beveled glass door and transoms.

The East End Historical District Association maintains a "pocket park" on this corner. It features one of seventeen water foundations "for both man and beasts" bequeathed by Henry Rosenberg's estate. Sculptor John Massey Rhind penned twelve watercolor designs, which were then constructed in 1898 of gray granite with bronze ornamentation. Many of them have been restored or reconstructed. This fountain was moved from 6th Street and Seawall Boulevard.

▶ Cross 15th St., continuing east.

1428 Ball Avenue

The first post-Victorian brick house built just prior to the 1900 Storm stands across 15th Street. A Prussian Jew and Texas' oldest jeweler, Michael W. Shaw added Tuscan columns to its massive entry so that this distinguished house upstages the others in this block. Notice the magnificent magnolias growing next door, thinned due to Ike.

1416 Ball Avenue

James Lykes, founder of the Lykes Brothers Steamship Company, built his home just prior to the birth of his son in 1908. Business demands moved the family to Houston in 1925.

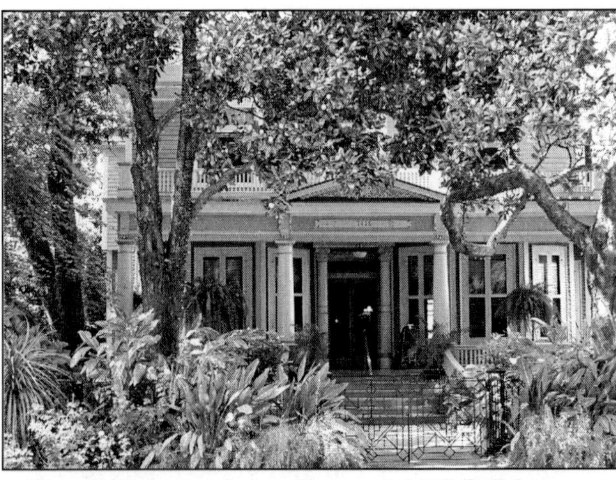

The 1908 James Lykes Home at 1416 Ball Avenue

1402 Ball Avenue

Shortly after the Civil War, George Fox joined his father's successful bakery, the Model Steam Bakery. He and his brother Chris were partners in 1903 when this house was built. George's stately mansion stands at the corner of 14th and Ball, replacing a house that was destroyed during the 1900 Storm. It combines the Queen Anne and Colonial Revival styles with a Victorian towered villa. Insurance records indicate that the double-galleried house on its west side was built in September 1897, when its second owner "took the cake rather than the whole (Model Steam) bakery."

1407 Ball Avenue

On the south side of the street, you'll walk past the Henry M. Stringfellow Home. Even though he earned his living in real estate and insurance, Stringfellow made his name as a horticulturist. He devised the "Oleander Plan": planting the fragrant flower along four sides of an Island garden to protect its crops within from the Gulf salt/sea breeze. In 1882, he moved his family to Hitchcock where he cultivated a pear orchard and Satsuma oranges which he had imported from Japan. After they moved back to Galveston, he built this north-facing wood-framed high Victorian home, then wrote *The New Horticulture* in 1896.

▶ Cross 14th St., staying on the south side.

1323 Ball Avenue

Note the simple cottage called the Miller-Jacobs Home. Built by the freight hauler, Ferdinand Miller in 1866, this side-hall plan home features pierced eaves for ventilation. Widow and prominent midwife, Barbara Lenz Jacobs, bought it in 1884.

1320 Ball Avenue

Look across the avenue at the Frederich-Erhard Victorian cottage. Built for the banker's family in 1894, its unique front stairs, featuring an intermediate landing and elaborate gingerbread, add drama to its entry. Also notice the sunburst motif in the gable. After Mr. Frederich died, his widow sold the house at to their nephew, Fred Erhard, in 1909. Mr. Erhard, who married Ollie Sims on June 9,1900, had established the printing and stationary firm of F. W. Erhard and Co. He died in San Antonio on June 7, 1934. The house remained in the family until 1972.

1316 Ball

The next three homes on the north side vary greatly. The 1895 Axel I. Roempke Home was built for the watchmaker, jeweler and optician. Its simple, vertical floor plan is made fancy by its recessed front porch to the west side.

1310 Ball Avenue

The large 1885 home of William H. Griffin has been conveniently divided into two residences both behind a common fence. Note the stained glass above the front doors: "L" for Left and "R" for Right.

1302 Ball Avenue

Coal dealer George D. Flood built the somber, stucco house on the corner in 1913. Note its windows.

1311 Ball Avenue

The houses on the south side of the avenue are awaiting rebirth by restoration, as reflected in this tiny cottage which has just been rehabilitated for entertaining.

1328 Ball Avenue

The grand Southern townhouse on the corner was built in 1868 for Charles Hurley, a prominent shipping and commission merchant in partnership with T. W. House. The home is easily distinguished by its two-story fluted Doric columns that lend a Greek Revival influence, and features a telescoping wing along its 14th Street side.

▶ 8 Cross Ball Avenue and retrace your steps back to 14th Street on the north side of the street.

811 14th Street

Look to the left in the middle of the previous block. Note the unusual entryway of the Traugott Schlueter-Blanton House. It is thought that Schlueter built the original part of this house in 1860, although insurance records do not show it until 1889. Builder Thomas Bludworth doubled its size and added the front stairway after he bought the home in 1945.

▶ ⑨ **Turn right at 14th Street, walking north.**

714 14th Street

Behind the Hurley home on the corner, this house dates to 1854 although it was completely remodeled in 1910.

615 and 613 14th Street

Within the next block on the west side of the street, please notice two small rental cottages.

Row Houses—608, 606 and 604 14th Street

Continuing on the east side, you'll walk past these three identical high-raised homes. Galveston's land speculators built duplicate, free-standing Row Houses as quick rental properties after the 1900 Storm, using two lots for three houses to maximize their investment.

▶ **Cross both 14th Street and Church Avenue.**

1401 Church Avenue

The William Werner Grocery Store, built in 1859, is one of the oldest surviving corner stores on the Island, originally remodeled in 1886. The two-story building with double galleries along 14th Street and bay windows on Church has recently been transformed into a beauty salon and barber shop.

1402 Church Avenue

The Herman B. Koppert Cottage was originally built at 906

30th Street around 1905 as one of two tenant houses. From a prestigious Jewish family, Kopperl's dad established the coffee trade between Rio de Janeiro and Galveston, while his mother, Isabella Dyer, was nicknamed the "Mother of Palms" for her replanting efforts after the city's Grade Raising. In 1972, Herman's son sold the twin cottages to St. John's Missionary Baptist Church; twenty years later, the church gave this one to the Galveston Historical Foundation, who restored it using materials salvaged from the other. After GHF moved it to the Church Street location, they sold the cottage in 1995.

1401 Postoffice Avenue

Around the corner, you'll find the final house on your two-part walk of Galveston's East End Historical District: West Side Wanderings and East Side Stories. Built in 1876 for a sea captain William Weber who never lived here, the dormered raised cottage changed hands frequently over the years—from one druggist to another in 1888, to a Danish seaman, until three Austrian brothers, partners in several restaurants, bought it in 1938. The cottage now houses a real estate office.

▶ ⑩ Cross 14th Street on Postoffice Avenue.

Back at your car, note the Mexican restaurant, Café and Bakery closely spaced along this well-trod street, once an ambulance route to UTMB. Consider ending your journey of the East End Historical District with a bite to eat at one of them!

CHAPTER 3

Broadway Promenade

FROM ITS INCEPTION, FASHIONABLE BROADWAY was designed to be the city's principle thoroughfare with its esplanade, precisely landscaped with live oaks, palms and oleanders. The Groesbeck survey allowed a width of 150 feet in 1838, making it the first divided boulevard in a Texas town. However, the name "Broadway Boulevard" just didn't stick to the city's official Avenue J, even though the City Council designated it so in August 1869. Twenty years later, the *Galveston Daily News* compared it to New York's Fifth Avenue, when Galveston's most prestigious neighborhood became known as the "Castle District." During the decadent decade of the 1890s, many of the Island's entrepreneurial elite built grand, towered palaces to celebrate their wealth. Streetcars ran its median until the avenue was paved in 1913 for automobile traffic. Fifteen years later, Broadway became the main entrance to the city when it connected with the new paved highway to Houston, Interstate 45, aka I 45. As the years passed, many of those majestic mansions were demolished, replaced by more modern structures, both commercial and residential. As a result, Broadway now reflects more than 140 years of popular architectural styles, from Antebellum Ashton Villa to the High Victorian Bishop's Palace, from Colonial Revivals to the more modest bungalows of the Roarin' Twenties—in a word: Eclectic!

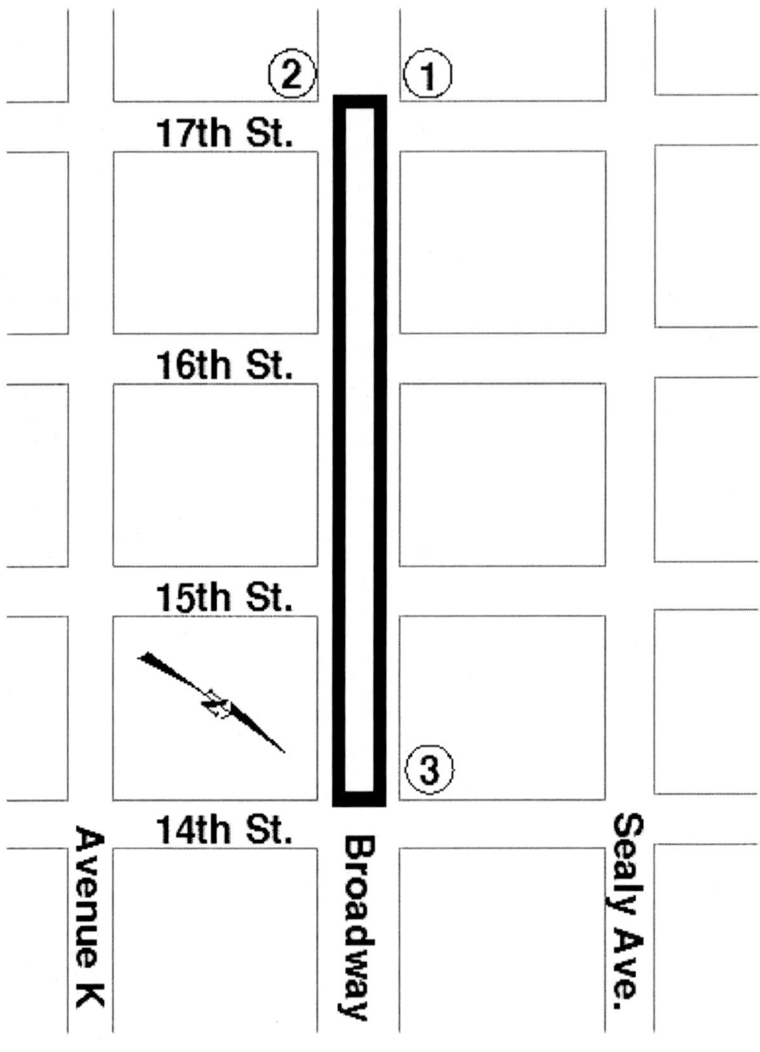

Broadway Promenade East

▶ ① Park your car on 17th St., north of Broadway preferably facing south. You'll follow the map of Broadway Promenade East .

1702–10 Broadway

Walking just half a block to the right will put you directly in front of the 1893 residence of wealthy real estate investor J. C. League. Designed by Nicholas Clayton, the League House features a fashionable porte-cochere to its east with Colonial Revival detail. The Leagues spared no expense in their extra large lot which includes a walled garden that extends to Sealy Avenue. Eliza Seinsheimer Kempner, widow of prominent city father Harris, lived here from 1919 to 1947, and added an enclosed garden room in 1920.

1721 Broadway

Looking south across Broadway in the middle of the block, note the simple Greek Revival raised cottage. The center portion of this house was moved from 14th and Broadway to make room for Walter Gresham's Castle in 1886. New owner Judge John Z. H. Scott hired Nicholas Clayton to enlarge it for his growing family. Actor Zachary Scott was his grandson.

John Z. H. Scott Home

1701–05 Broadway

The imposing 1914 John Adriance Home stands on the corner. Designed by Houston architect Lewis S. Green, this Colonial Revival incorporates a Craftsman gable and a wrap-around porch with massive Doric columns in its entry and a porte cochere on its west side. A partner in the Trueheart real estate brokerage, Adriance sold the house to civic leader Oscar Springer in 1929, who maintained the home until 1960.

▶ **2 Cross Broadway at the corner and turn left, walking east.**

1623 Broadway

Built circa 1868, this updated Victorian cottage resembles Greek Revival, in miniature. Note its twin attic dormers.

1607 Broadway

In contrast, the straight-lined symmetry of this home was designed in 1940 by Houston architect Ben Milam for the Robert E. Oldfields. It was the first slab-on-grade foundation built on Galveston Island.

▶ **Cross 16th Street.**

1527 Broadway

The Joseph Lobit mansion filled half of this block of Broadway until it was demolished in 1920. Attorney-to-be-Judge Jules Damiani purchased the corner lot and hired Raymond Rapp, an architect newly-arrived from Kentucky, to build this relatively simple stucco bungalow on the corner in 1921.

1521 Broadway

Rapp also designed the brick bungalow next door for executive grocer Peter Gengler in 1925. Originally German immigrants, he and his brother, John, started from a horse-cart in 1851. At Market and 20th Street, the second oldest grocery store in the US celebrated its Diamond Anniversary the year after this home

16th and Broadway

1871 Archibald Campbell house

was built. Note the small entry porches, hipped roof and rectangular floor plans of both this and the Damiani home on the corner.

1515 Broadway
First built in 1871 by Archibald Campbell of the Mallory Line, the house reflects an "American Southern Victorian" style. Its various curving gingerbread more accurately reflects its remodeling of 1888, perhaps the work of the German architect, Alfred Muller.

1509 Broadway

Although merchant John S. Rhea built the Greek Revival cottage as rental property, he sold it to John Hertford in 1867. When his son defaulted in 1899 to Theodore Ohmstede, Della and Michael Collerain bought the house in 1905. Collerain and his brother, Patrick, owned the Brick Wharf Saloon on Pier 20 until Michael became a city policeman.

The doctor's clinic on the corner replaced the 1871 J. D. Skinner home in 1960.

▶ Cross 15th Street.

1425 Broadway

The congregation of St. Paul's United Methodist Church traces its roots to one of the oldest African American churches in Texas, until it split over the name of Reedy AME Chapel. You will pass this church later during your Broadway Promenade. C. W. Bulger designed the Gothic Revival St. Paul's, with an obligatory Victorian corner tower and spire in 1902, as a replacement for the original church at 8th and Ball which was destroyed during the 1900 Storm. The next two homes survived that Great Storm.

1407–09 Broadway

British-born Thomas Lucas built his original Terrace Row at 6th and Broadway, facing the beach. After it was totally destroyed during the 1900 Storm, he salvaged the brick to rebuild these Lucas Terrace Apartments at the site of his own home, completing the project in 1908. Unique to his design is the open, curving stairways and concrete planter boxes.

1403 Broadway

The Powhatan L. Wren Home on the corner was originally built in 1873 as a simple cottage by Edward Sylvester. He sold it in 1885 to Mr. Wren, a city clerk who rose to the deputy collector of customs and finally city alderman. He hired Robert B. Garrett to substantially rebuild the cottage to accommodate his family of six. Raising it four feet, Garrett enclosed the front porches and added four second-floor dormers, the back porch and the square bay window over the entry. It was lovingly landscaped and restored in 1997.

 **Cross Broadway at 14th Street Turn left, walking west.**

928 14th Street

The bright white Sacred Heart Church dominates the northeast corner. Nicholas Clayton's original 1892 High Victorian Romanesque design minus its ornate dome fronted Broadway in the middle of the block. During the 1900 Storm, debris from wood-framed houses, driven by the raging water, literally battered down that entry. A photo of the devastation hangs inside the church beneath a life-sized crucifix which survived along with two small stained-glass windows above the altar. Today's Scared Heart was designed by a Jesuit brother named Jimenez. Consecrated in 1904, the exterior design was based on Notre Dame in Paris because France helped finance its construction. He also borrowed elements from "Puerto Santa Maria" in Toledo, Spain, which was originally built as a Grand Synagogue to incorporate Moorish, Byzantine, Gothic, and Romanesque design influences. Although disappointed not to win Sacred Heart's reconstruction, Clayton did design its "onion" dome in 1915, thought to be his final project. Interestingly enough, his declined drawings were pirated by another Jesuit, Brother Otten, who used them for a church in Augusta, Georgia. That building still stands today, as a well maintained cultural center. The Rectory at 13th and Broadway was designed in 1925 by Raymond Rapp.

1402 Broadway

The grandest mansion on Broadway, now known as the Bishop's Palace, was originally built as the Walter Gresham Castle in 1886. After moving a smaller house to 1721 Broadway, the lawyer-politician-legislator hired Clayton to design his house. The public was officially welcomed on New Year's Day, 1893. Built of Texas pink granite, sandstone and limestone, his castle cost a reported $250,000. Elements of Romanesque, Queen Ann and Renaissance with angels literally carved in stone make this High Victorian an almost over-the-top extreme.

Over the years, Gresham collected fireplaces, storing them until he built his dream home. Placing each in a room of its own, Clayton designed the room around the fireplace. The Music Room still features a most unusual one made of silver and onyx, which won an award at the 1886 New Orleans World's Fair.

In 1923, the family sold the castle to the Galveston/Houston Catholic Diocese for $40,500. Bishop Christopher Byrne lived here until his death in 1950. After the Diocese was moved to Houston, the castle/palace was restored and opened to the public as Galveston's first house museum in 1963. Today, it is valued in excess of $7 million. The Bishop's Palace is one of 14 Best Representative Homes of the Victorian Era as well as one of the 100 Best Built Homes in the U.S, as complied by the American Institute of Architects—the only home in Texas to be listed on both.

1416 Broadway

Next door, Clayton designed an equally grand home for Mr. and Mrs. Sylvain Blum in June 1885. Unfortunately, it was demol-

Gresham Castle, Blum and Trueheart Mansions
—From author's collection of postcards

ished in 1915. Anton F. Korn designed two houses to replace it for business partners Carl Biehl and Richard B. Wilkens. Biehl married Hilda Reymershoffer, whose family owned the Texas Star Flour Mill. This house remains in the Biehl family.

1428 Broadway

The Wilkens Home on the corner was built in 1916 by Richard and his wife, Olga. Incorporating elements of Colonial Revival with Neo-Classical, this expansive English country house features Doric columns in its entry. Architect Louis Oliver used its raised basement as his office from 1966 until 1994.

1502 Broadway

The Isaac H. Kempner Home stands proudly on this northwest corner of Broadway. Instrumental in the city's recovery after the 1900 Storm, Kempner married Henrietta Blum in 1902, and commissioned C. W. Bulger to design this house, which was completed in 1906. Neoclassical and Colonial Revival on the outside, its original interior design is truly eclectic, mixing Federal, Prairie and Craftsman. It was made more so in 1924 when Houston architect John F. Staub added a west wing. The house remained in the Kempner family until 1970, changing hands several times until 1983, when Mary Moody Northen moved in, ending her life here three years later at the age of 94.

The deep-set house next door, which is still in the Kempner family, began as a servant's apartment over the garage. It was enlarged several times during the 1940s and '50s. The empty lot on the corner was once occupied by the 1876 Sawyer/Flood house, which was demolished in 1965.

▶ **Cross 16th Street.**

1602 Broadway

Also on a par with Walter Gresham's castle was that of real estate broker Henry Trueheart. The two-and-one-half story mansion—complete with a four-story tower, carriage house and gardens—filled most of this northwest block at 16th and Broadway.

In 1928, his widow and daughter, Sally, decided that it was

too much house to maintain. The lot was subdivided and the corner property sold to Dr. Albert Singleton, a surgery professor at UTMB. He hired Cameron Fairchild to design his Monterey style home in 1931, even though the original Trueheart black-and-red checkered sidewalk remains today. Although hidden by a tall brick wall, the two-story house features a double veranda and red tiled roof. An accomplished mural artist, Mrs. Joan Singleton's artwork remains in the house and has been carefully preserved.

1616 Broadway

Three years earlier, the Trueheart ladies had commissioned architect Fairchild, who made his mark in Houston's River Oaks, to build them a smaller home in the garden—a Mediterranean design reminiscent of the pink "Hollywood Hills" homes of the Roarin' Twenties. Note the mansion's original driveway leading to the porte cochere over the west side entry and the original carriage house behind—a 1900 Storm survivor, which now houses an art studio.

▶ **Arriving back at your car on 17th Street, turn right to drive west on Broadway to 23rd (aka Tremont) Street. The map will not reflect these driving instructions.**

Many other homes were sacrificed for commercial development on the north side of the street. This includes the 1889 Morris Lasker House, 1728 Broadway, which was said to be Nicholas Clayton's grandest residential design. This home was demolished in 1967.

However, there are several structures of note on the south side of Broadway, in particular between 18th and 19th Streets. As you drive to 23rd Street, note these houses. If you prefer, walk the 1800 block for a closer look.

1805 Broadway

The Thomas E. Bailey Home was designed for the general manger of the Galveston Wharf Company in 1893 by H. C. Cooke before he moved his architectural firm to Houston.

1809 Broadway

Next door is the1889 Justus J. Schott Home. This druggist who is credited with inventing chewing gum built this house as rental property, eventually for his Assistant Manager. The next two houses were built in 1887. Lawyer Henry J. Labatt built **1815 Broadway**, while the house next door with its unique gingerbread trim was built for Mrs. M. F. Talfor.

2013 Broadway

Two blocks west on the south side of Broadway stands the first African Methodist Episcopal Church in Texas. Originally established as the "Negro Church" for their slaves in 1848, the Methodist masters deeded the land at 20th and Broadway to them in 1867. Named for its second pastor, the 1886 Reedy Chapel replaced the original church which was destroyed in the 1885 fire. Note the pyramid-roofed tower of this Gothic design by Benjamin G. Chisolm. In 1913, the congregation bought a used organ from Henry Pilcher and Sons, which had originally been built for Galveston's Trinity Episcopal Church in 1872. Today, it is the only tracker organ of its type still in use in the United States; the other sits in the Smithsonian.

2217 Broadway

Just before you turn right on 23rd Street, you may notice the John Francis Smith House in the middle of the block. Built in 1884, this Italianate townhouse features a bay window balcony, the original iron fence and tiled sidewalk.

▶ ④ Turn right onto 23rd St., then left into the parking lot on Sealy Avenue. Park your car here. Follow the West map of the Broadway Promenade (on the next page).

823 23rd Street

Note the green tiled hipped roof of the Rosenberg Library. Chartered in 1871 as the Galveston Mercantile Library, the city boasted the oldest public library in the state, but it did not have a place for its collection until Swiss immigrant, Henry Rosenberg, bequeathed $400,000 to construct this building. Eames and Young of St. Louis won the architectural competition in October 1901, and designed this Italian Renaissance/French Beaux-Arts structure which opened in 1904. Note its terra cotta panels inscribed with the names of great writers. The bronze statue of Mr. Rosenberg guards the original entrance. The Moody Memorial Wing opened in 1971, effectively changing the address to 2310 Sealy. Galveston's Rosenberg Library remains one of the first generation of public libraries still in use today.

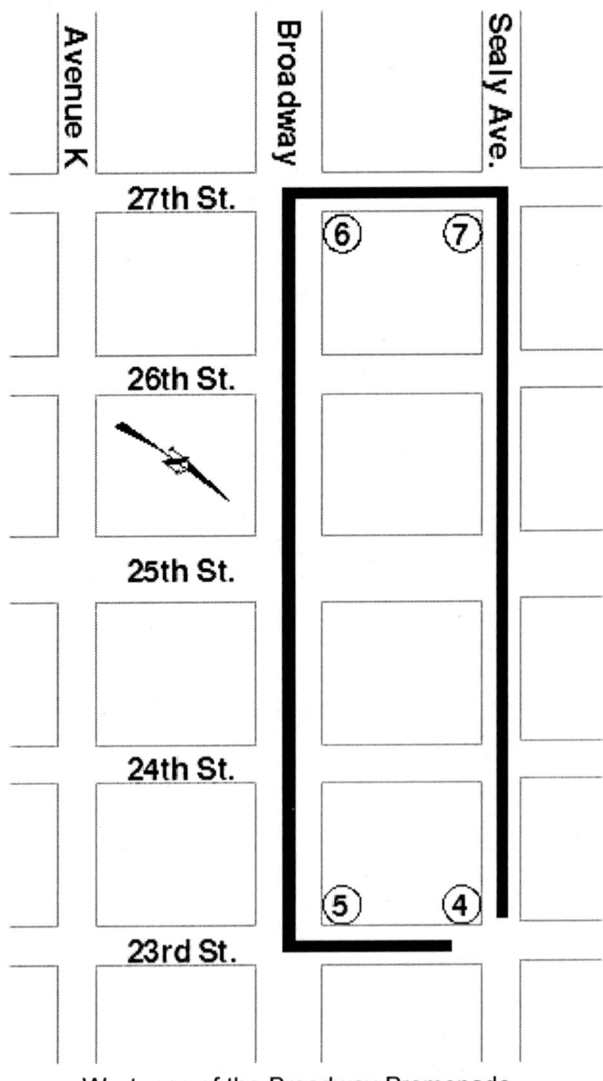

West map of the Broadway Promenade

▶ 5 Walk to Broadway alongside or through the Harris Garden and turn right. Continue your exploration westward.

The Sealy-Smith Foundation replaced the circa 1890 P. J. Willis home with a Firestone Tire outlet in 1952. In 1997, the Galveston Foundation funded an urban retreat, the Harris Garden, on this corner. In memory of his parents, John W. and Minnie Hutching Harris, son John dedicated the park, "For the Use and Enjoyment of the Citizens of Galveston and Visitors to the Island." An artful Pergola, lighted in purplish blue and encircled by a brick pathway, provides the focal aesthetic feature.

The large statue outside the garden is a recent addition. Of no one in particular, it commemorates the day that the 1863 Emancipation Proclamation ended slavery in the south: June 19, 1865. "Juneteenth" became an official Texas holiday in 1979.

Harris Garden Pergola

2328 Broadway

Built and designed by hardware merchant James Moreau Brown in 1859, this home set a precedent as the first fashionable house on Broadway. Since he didn't want it called the "Brown House," he borrowed his wife's mother's maiden name, Ashton and, combined with its Italianate style, he christened it Ashton Villa. This three-story red brick mansion was scheduled to be demolished in 1969 when local historical preservationists persuaded the city to buy it with funds from the Department of Housing and Urban Development. The Galveston Historical Foundation restored it and maintains it as a house museum, but still leases it from the city. Most of the more colorful stories surrounding Ashton Villa center upon Mr. Brown's very lovely, redheaded daughter, Rebecca, who is affectionately known as Miss Betty. She never married but literally devoted her life to art. Many of her "risqué" pastel paintings on corduroy are still in residence at Ashton Villa.

▶ **Cross 24th Street.**

2424 Broadway

The original site of the E. B. Nichols family home became Open Gates, named for the ornate, wrought-iron entry of the 1889 George Sealy Mansion. A successful banker and City Father, Sealy sent his wife, formerly Magnolia Willis, to New York in 1886 to hire "the finest architect" to design a home for their family of eight. The result was Stanford White's imposing Neo-Renaissance with Italianate details, complete with cherry wood bookcases in the library, a ballroom with an acoustically appropriate curved ceiling and a small stage in the attic for family plays. Nicholas Clayton, who supervised the construction, designed the Romanesque carriage house two years later. In 1979, the family gave the house to the University of Texas Medical Branch, which restored it with private donations. Open Gates now serves as their teleconferencing center and is not open to the public.

Dramatically marking the intersection of 25th Street (aka Rosenberg) and Broadway is the Texas Heroes Monument, another gift from the estate of Henry Rosenberg. Dedicated to the men who fought and died in the 1836 Texas Revolution against Mexico, the bronze statue of Victory stands atop a granite pedestal, 72 feet above the ground. Designed by Italian Louis Amateis, the monument was dedicated on San Jacinto Day, April 21, 1900, the same day that 25th Street was officially renamed Rosenberg.

Open Gates

Texas Heroes Monument
—From author's collection

A closer view of the bronze statue, Victory, atop the monument.

▶ Cross both 25th and 26th Streets, walking two blocks west.

2618 Broadway

Built in 1895 by Narcissa Willis after her husband died, this Romanesque 31-room showplace was designed by British architect, William H. Tyndall. Of particular note are its pyramidal roof, tower arrangement, and dormer window, which were reminiscent of the Vanderbilt mansion in New York City. During construction, one of the stone arches fell, killing the chief mason, Richard Fealey. Reportedly, most of the $125,000 cost went toward the grand interiors by Pottier & Stymus of New York. Each room on the first floor reflects a different style, but its centerpiece is a stained-glass window above the grand staircase inscribed, "Welcome Ever Smiles." Unfortunately, Mrs. Willis died in 1899, and her daughter who lived in New York, sold the house after the 1900 Storm to W. L. Moody, Jr., for $20,000. It took seven years and over $10 million to restore the home, which is now open as a house museum. In 1997, both it and the Bishop's Palace were featured on an A&E's "America's Castles."

To accomplish the restoration, the late Mary Moody Northen established her own foundation. Its offices are housed in the raised cottage on the corner, built in 1867 by grocer William P. Quigg. Ten years later, he sold it to Victor J. Baulard, a Frenchman who had immigrated in 1845 and made full partner in a paint, oils and glass company. He added the front bay windows in 1887.

All three Broadway Beauties—the Moody Mansion, Ashton Villa and the Bishop's Palace—can be toured in a money-saving package, available at any one of the three.

▶ 6 Turn right on 27th Street.

▶ 7 Turn right again on Sealy Avenue, walking east.

823 Rosenberg

On your way back to your car, you will pass the central fire station, which replaced the Old City Auditorium in 1965 after it was badly damaged in Hurricane Carla four years earlier. Note the adjoining City Hall that faces 25th Street, built in 1916.

From this perspective, you can see the second floor balconies of the Sealy Mansion through the trees. Sealy's eldest daughter, Margaret, wrote that her mother pulled many people to safety from here during the 1900 Storm. As many as 400 people survived the storm in the Sealy mansion, including workmen and sailors.

▶ **Cross 25th Street.**

Behind Open Gates on the corner of 25th and Sealy stands an oleander bush reported to be an offshoot of the original. In 1841, importer Joseph Osterman brought a cutting of the tropical plant from Jamaica back to his sister, Mrs. Rosanna Dyer, who lived in this block. It flourished in the salt/sea air of Galveston Island, which soon became known as the "Oleander City." The bushes' fragrant flowers bloom profusely every spring in varying shades of white, pink, and yellow, both single and double. Be warned, however—its sap can be poisonous!!

Passing behind Ashton Villa, notice the modern Moody Memorial Wing of the Rosenberg Library across Sealy Avenue, designed by Galveston architect Thomas Price. This wing houses the Galveston and Texas History Center on its third floor, with its extensive collection of historic documents, manuscripts, photographs and ephemera of the city's founding fathers.

▶ **Finding yourself at your car means you have finished your Broadway Promenade.**

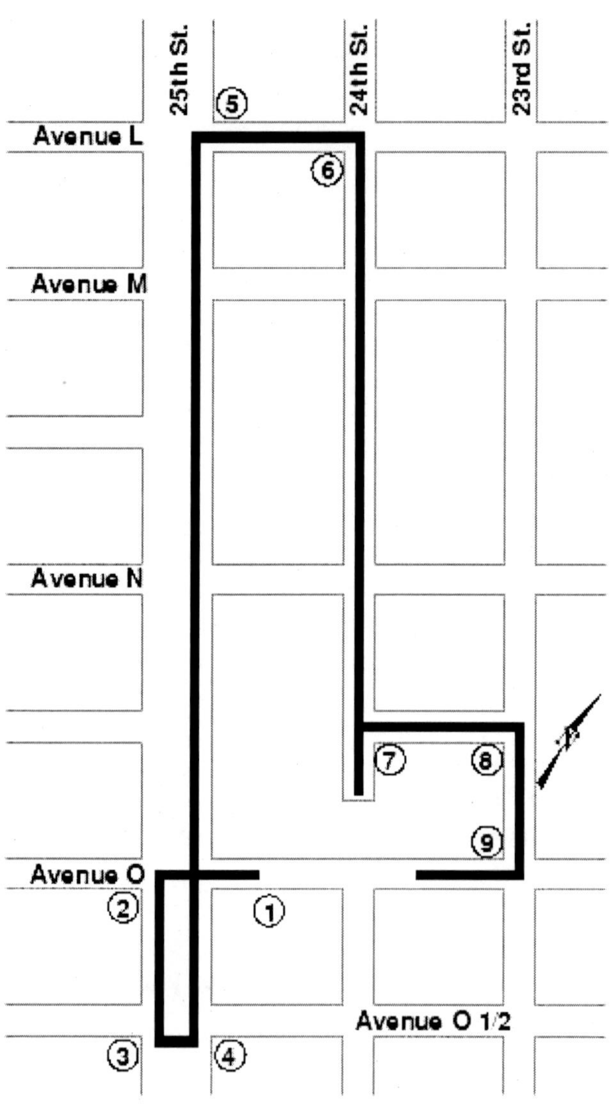

Map of the Silk Stocking Stroll

CHAPTER 4

Silk Stocking Stroll

ALTHOUGH FIRST ORGANIZED IN 1975, the Silk Stocking Historic District wasn't officially listed on the National Register of Historic Places until 1996. The neighborhood features some of Galveston's best Queen Anne designs even though its homes date from the 1860s through the Roarin' Twenties. The District, which includes four complete square blocks and portions of twelve others, takes its name from a sign of affluence at the turn of the 20th century, as it was said that only those who could afford real silk stockings could afford to live here.

From 1871, the Texas Cotton Press and Manufacturing Company stood behind a wall on the three-block outlot between 24th and 25th Streets, with north-south borders Avenues M and N. A railroad line ran east to west along the latter. In 1890, the Texas Railroad Commission decided that all cotton grown in the state must be pressed closer to its home. This ruling put the Cotton Press out of business in 1891, when the building was torn down. The land was subdivided into 32 narrow lots and sold at public auction in December 1898. Land speculators invested for development of middle-class housing. Only five houses on the original outlot were completed before the 1900 Storm. Development on adjacent streets began in 1905.

Complete with an esplanade, which is planted with palms, magnolias and oleanders, the Groesbeck's original major north/south thoroughfare, 25th Street, connected the central business district with the beach front. It was originally called Bath Avenue for the number of bath houses located at its Gulf of Mexico base. At the dedication of the Texas Heroes Monument on April 21, 1900, its name was changed to Rosenberg to honor the city's biggest benefactor, the diminutive Swiss immigrant, Henry Rosenberg. You'll find both designations for this street interchanged in this chapter, with the number used for directions and the name, for addresses.

Coming to Galveston in 1842, Rosenberg began working as a clerk in a dry goods shop. Within four years, he owned the business, which he grew into the state's leading dry goods store by 1859. Perhaps the city's best success story, he invested in the Island's business district and owned several buildings on The Strand. In 1882, he partially endowed Trinity Episcopal's fellowship hall, named after its first rector, Benjamin Eaton. Four years later, Rosenberg funded a public elementary school. After he died in 1893, his estate granted over a million dollars for very specific projects throughout the city, all built between 1895 and 1905. The single largest amount of $400,000 went toward a public library at 23rd and Sealy. He also left $35,000 to build Grace Episcopal Church at 36th and Avenue L as well as seventeen water fountains "for both men and beasts" scattered throughout the city's east end. Another of his gifts was the Letitia Rosenberg Home for Women, which you will see further south on this street.

▶ ❶ Park your car on Avenue O, on the east side of 25th St., aka Rosenberg Avenue.

2419 Avenue O

Note the raised Victorian cottage behind the trees. Built in 1892 for Frederick M. Gilbough, who worked for the Gulf, Colorado & Santa Fe Railroad, its tall orientation is topped by a peaked roof line. The house next door was part of the Predicki family rental property on the corner.

▶ ❷ Cross 25th Street at the light and turn left, walking south on the west side of the street.

Serving as the border between two neighborhoods, this intersection bears a decorative brown street sign marking it as the Kempner Park Neighborhood. The three plain, wood-framed houses on the southwest corner are recent construction. However, the four houses to their immediate south were built either in 1914 or 1915 and are considered part of the Silk Stocking District.

1719 Rosenberg

This brick bungalow upstages the house to its north. Reflecting the Prairie style, it features a gable—an inverted triangle formed by two sloping planes of the roof.

1723 Rosenberg

The stuccoed Mediterranean on the corner features a colonnaded front porch, which was originally screened, creating a second floor balcony for owners, Dr. and Mrs. Henry C. Haden. This house is now a Bed and Breakfast.

▶ ❸ Cross both 25th Street and Avenue O ½ for closer look at the next magnificent mansion.

1804 Rosenberg

The Letitia Rosenberg Home for Women dominates the block of Avenue O ½ at 25th Street. A graduate of the royal Academy of Fine Arts in Berlin, German architect Alfred Muller designed an imposing Renaissance Revival for twenty prominent Galveston widows in 1895,

The Letitia Rosenberg Home for Women

a gift from Henry Rosenberg's estate, in memory of his first wife. Its main staircase is encased in its original octagonal tower, even though its exterior has been much altered due to storm damage over the years. Closing in 1970, the house bore its name across its roofline, until recently restored. It now crowns the media room inside.

▶ ❹ Turn to the right and walk north on 25th Street.

1710 and 1706 Rosenberg

At the corner of Avenue O stand two simple Craftsman style wood-frame houses that were rental homes built by Isadore Predicki and his two single sisters in 1913. Their investment included the home around the corner. They lived in their father's house further north down the street.

Even though it is definitely part of the Kempner Park Neighborhood, the perspective of green palms against the rosy stucco and red tiled roof of the Daniel Webster Kempner Home is so much more dramatic from this side of the esplanade!

2504 Avenue O

This graceful Mission Revivial style country home sits discretely behind a tall, stucco wall. The second son of Harris and Eliza Kempner, D. W. bought the property on Avenue O, 25th to 27th Streets, from the Ursuline Sisters. He chose these three lots for his house and gardens, designed by Mauran, Russell and Garden of St. Louis. D. W. married Jeane Bertig on June 6, 1906, and construction on their home started soon after their honeymoon was over. Completed in 1910, it actually reflects a combination Mission Revival, Spanish Colonial, and Mediterranean styles. D. W. sold the rest of the land to friends and family, thereby assuring the quality of the neighborhood. Actively serving on the boards of all the family businesses, Kempner spearheaded the beachfront Hotel Galvez project in 1911.

2428 Avenue O

Back on the east side of Rosenberg, Stowe and Stowe designed this massive Prairie style home for lawyer William T. Armstrong III in 1914. His wife, Josephine, was Walter Gresham's daughter.

Directly behind the Kempner house across the esplanade once stood the Ursuline Convent. On January 19, 1847, seven sisters from the New Orleans order arrived on Galveston Island at the request of Bishop Jean Marie Odin of St. Mary's Cathedral. Using the former home of Judge James Love, they quickly established a convent and academy. In 1891, Nicholas Clayton designed a magnificent High Victorian Venetian Gothic structure—his masterpiece, some speculate. So heavily damaged during 1961's Hurricane Carla, it was finally demolished in 1974. There is part of its original brick wall separating its property from the Kempner home. Galveston Catholic School, grades K–8, now stands here. In tribute, Avenue N is sometimes referred to as Ursuline.

The Ursuline Convent

—From the author's collection of postcards

1602 Rosenberg

This suburban chalet was built in 1925 for bagging company owner, Joseph Swiff. Also called Mission Revival, the house features a gabled roof above its entry.

1520, 1512 Rosenberg

The raised cottages and bungalows in the 1500 block of 25th Street were built between 1905 and 1925 and range in style from Colonial Revival to Queen Anne. In particular, note the 1922 bungalow at **1520 Rosenberg** and the Queen Anne, built in 1906, at **1512**.

1502 Rosenberg

The 1929 familiar townhouse-style on the corner, called Colonial Revival, sits flush against the front sidewalk.

▶Crossing Avenue N, continue walking north down 25th Street.

1423 Rosenberg

Across the esplanade, Silk Stocking developer Tim Sullivan lived on the corner of Avenue N. He built several homes on 24th Street as rental properties. You'll see many Queen Anne designs on the west side of this block across 25th Street, all built between 1900 and 1908.

1422 Rosenberg

Authors Beasley and Fox of the *Galveston Architectural Guide* suggested that the next three homes were dramatically Southern Victorian, "something Tennessee Williams might have imagined." Most were thought to be designs by C. W. Bulger. This Classical Revival was the youngest of the two-story wood-frame houses, built in 1910.

1420 and 1414 Rosenberg

The next two gabled Queen Annes were probably built as rentals in 1899. The Victorian chalet with Queen Anne elements was built by developer Gustav Kahn. A Mrs. Marie Buechner originally built its neighbor to the north, which was vastly improved in 1907 by its second owner, Lawrence P. Dignan. Note the delightful roof details and gingerbread

1412 Rosenberg

Another middle class tenant home stands next door. Seemingly however, George H. Nicholls spared no expense in its craftsmanship, especially in the staircase. All of the woodwork is pine and the stained glass is original. Banker Fred W. Catterall eventually made his home here.

1406 Rosenberg

William R. White of the Southern Coffee Company, built this Queen Anne in 1899.

1400 Rosenberg

Samuel Levine, who worked in the cotton industry, built this house that same year, soon selling it to H. H. Haines who used it as rental property. According to the current owner, a couple of guardian spirits have been sighted—a short older man wearing dark blue baggy pants in the dining room and, upstairs in the front bedroom, a tall woman. He was deaf while she was both deaf and dumb. It seems as though the lady who lived here at the turn of the century took in just such a couple after their families perished during the 1900 Storm. The ghosts have since moved on, leaving behind parting gifts of gratitude on a Sunday morning—a checker board and a small Singer sewing machine.

1322 Rosenberg

Prussian immigrant, Jacob Predecki, built this Queen Anne with its generous wrap-around verandas in 1903. He and his wife, Emma, had four children, 1 boy and 3 girls, none of whom ever

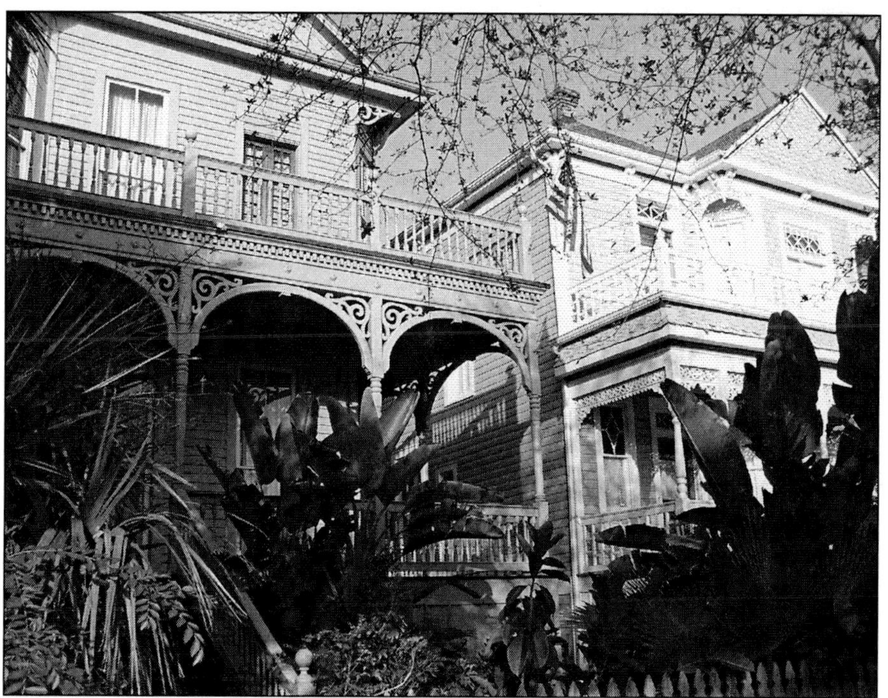

1400, 1406 Rosenberg

married. While daughter Selma moved to Kerrville, son Isadore and his sisters Rosa and Gertrude lived here for 63 years, when the latter passed away in 1966. Isadore supported them all as a cashier, then bookkeeper for the Galveston Shoe and Hat Company. In 1913, he bought property from John Sealy further south on 25th Street to build three rental houses.

Predecki home

1320 Rosenberg

Luther Murff built this double-galleried frame home in September, 1899. The Great Storm of 1900 blew it off its original foundation, which was repaired by December of that year. He sold it to roofer John George in 1905, who then sold it to James E. Marable twenty years later. The family of this Galveston Wharves master mechanic lived here for fifty years.

1311 Rosenberg

Across the esplanade, parallel with 1310, stands the Oscar A. Walker Home. Walker, a clerk in several Galveston dry goods stores, built his home here in 1904. His son continued to live here for forty years. Even though its original architecture was altered over the years, the house still retains much of its gingerbread as well as its floor to 11-foot ceiling windows.

▶ Cross Avenue M.

1208 Rosenberg

Among newer construction in the next block, you'll past the unique John H. Moser House. Originally built in 1859 at another location, this small raised cottage was moved and rebuilt in 1885 by the marble cutter. Moser had moved his tombstone and monument shop next door by 1888, which has become its fenced garden today. Other members of the Moser family lived around the corner on the south side of Avenue L.

1213 Rosenberg

Across the esplanade stands this Prairie style home. Built in 1913 by a Dr. Brett, it soon sold to sea captain, Mark Dierlam. He and his wife, Gladys, raised a son and daughter here. Mark Jr. recalled that his family stayed home during Hurricane Carla in 1961, playing bridge to pass the time. An avid golfer to the end, his mom died at age 101.

▶ ❺ Cross Avenue L and turn right, walking east on the north side of the street.

2428 Avenue L

At the corner of 25th and Avenue L stands the Vaiani Store. Typical of corner-store buildings on Galveston Island, Emily Irving owned the original 1890 two-story Queen Anne residence until 1901. Grocer Albert Vaiani added the commercial space and canopy in 1913.

2424 Avenue L

In 1884, Bavarian immigrant Adloph Frenkel bought the first of three identical tenant houses built by the Galveston Real Estate and Loan Association a year earlier. Immediately, he added two rooms to accommodate his family, and had the house wired for electricity. After his death in 1921 at age 82, they continued to live here until 1945, when it changed hands many times as rental property until it was renovated in 1993. The third house is barely recognizable as one of triplets.

2410 Avenue L

Three doors down, the neo-Georgian country house with its circular driveway stands out among the Victorians. It was designed by Houston architect John Staub in 1927 for insurance executive Clinton G. Wells, Jr.

2419 Avenue L

Look across Avenue L to see three other Moser homes. John's single sister, Miss Paula, owned this 1896 Victorian raised cottage. Agnes Moser and her husband, John Roemer, who owned the Sunny South Saloon, built the gabled house next door, which was designed by John Hourigan in May of 1888. Its plainer twin was built next door a year later as rental income for her mother, Eliza.

2402 Avenue L

James Moreau Brown of Ashton Villa, two blocks north on Broadway, gave his younger daughter, Matilda, this ornate raised cottage when she married Thomas H. Sweeney in 1885. Its design, most likely by Alfred Muller, suggests a nautical theme, especially in its dormer windows that protrude like the bow of a ship in its Eastlake detailing. Matilda and her children moved out before her 1896 divorce from Sweeney, who turned out to be a drunken and very abusive husband.

Sweeney-Royston House

In 1911, Judge Mart H. Royston moved into the cottage, and lived here until his death in 1948.

1124 24th Street

Another magnificent house stands across 24th Street on the opposite corner. Brother to Texas' Reconstruction governor and president of the Galveston Wharf Board, Waters Davis built this large combination of Italianate and Queen Anne styles in 1868. Note its single story wrap-around veranda and tower. The house served as the headquarters of the American Red Cross, which the Davis family had helped to establish, from 1945 until 1977. It was restored into a single family dwelling in 1986. The house and garden on its north side belonged to the Davis' daughter, Sarah and husband, Harry Hawley.

The Waters Davis House

2323 Avenue L

Across the street from the Waters Davis House is a Queen Anne design built in 1890.

▶ ⑥ Turn right on 24th St., walking south on the west side of the street.

1201, 1214 24th Street

Among the newer homes in the next block, you'll pass an 1895 raised cottage at **1201 24th Street** as well as a 1900 bungalow across the street at **1214**.

24th Street Cottages

2327 Avenue M

The 1893 Hickenlooper House stands on the corner. Daughter Lucy grew up here from 1893 to 1900 before achieving fame as concert pianist, Madame Olga Samaroff, the first American woman to teach at Julliard School of Music. She also married—and divorced—renowned symphony conductor, Leopold Stokowski.

2326–18 Avenue M

Across the avenue, these Greek Revival Gulf Coast cottages

date from 1870 and were rented to African American domestics, cooks and waiters.

▶Cross Avenue M.

1303 24th Street

One of the first homes built on the original Texas Cotton Press site stands on the corner, a Queen Anne built in 1898 for three single sisters.

1305 24th Street

Next door, note the windows of the 1908 Southern townhouse which was owned by Mrs. Annie Chapman. Its neighbor to the south was built that same year.

1315 24th Street

In 1899, reporter Nat Davis, who wrote the earliest account of the Great 1900 Storm, commissioned C. W. Bulger to build a two story, galleried house. Ironically, Davis drowned two years later. That same year, entrepreneur Harry S. Spangler also hired Bulger to design his house next door at **1317**.

1319 24th Street

The 1899 E. R. Cheesborough Home was designed by George Stowe for this secretary-treasurer of the Texas Portland Cement and Lime Company. The house features a square side veranda to the south on its first floor, similar to those found in Charleston, North Carolina. Cheesborough would become the secretary of Galveston's Grade Raising Board after the 1900 Storm, which architectural historian Ellen Beasley has noted as "one of the most complicated projects ever undertaken by a community anywhere."

1325 24th Street

Contractor Fred Hartel, whose roofing company is still in business today, bought a lot and one-half for his family home in 1906. Designed by Charles F. Schelewa, this Colonial Revival features an arched window in its attic gable. After changing hands three times, the house stood vacant for 10 years and finally sold in 1992 at a tax foreclosure sale.

1329 24th Street

Thomas B. Dindale designed this home in 1899 for jeweler August F. Lange. It features an arched half-round window.

Most of the less grand houses on the east side of 24th Street, built between 1893 and 1898, show what a little paint in the right places can achieve. Next to a two story at **1318**, note the two raised cottages at **1322** and **1326 24th Street**, built in 1895. What these two tenant cottages lack in size they make up for in gingerbread detail.

1402 24th Street

This Queen Anne design features a peaked roof and stained glass panels around its windows. Its neighbor to the south is a two-story Colonial Revival complete with columns which was built in 1909.

1410 24th Street

The raised Victorian cottage shows off with a bay off its front porch and fancy fish scale siding on its roof.

1410 24th Street

1405 24th Street

Greek Revival in style, the George Ball home featured massive Doric columns and cornice. The banker originally built his stately home at the corner of 23rd (or Tremont) and Sealy in 1857. In 1902, John Focke bought it and had it moved to its present location to make way for the

The George Ball House and Wing

Rosenberg Library. The rather plain-faced house on its north side was originally its rear addition, a wing that was designed in 1882 by Joseph Goldthwaite.

1411 24th Street

Note the stained glass door panels in the 1903 Raised Cottage.

1417 24th Street

W. H. Tyndall designed this Queen Anne for real estate agent William S. Conness. With much gingerbread on its double galleries, its half-round front window lends a touch of elegance.

1421 24th Street

The Colonial Revival next door was built as rental property by Tim Sullivan in 1908. His first tenant was insurance executive J. Fellman Seinsheimer.

The house on the northwest corner of 24th and Avenue N is one of three row houses also built by Sullivan several years earlier. Each has been remodeled over the years, but **2408 Avenue N** still maintains most of their original design.

2328 Avenue N

The corner house across 24th Street was one of three Queen Anne "speculative houses" designed by C. W. Bulger in 1905 for Gustav Kahn.

▶ Cross Avenue N and continue walking south on 24th Street.

2401 Avenue N

Built in 1921, this Colonial Revival features a sloping mansard roof.

With irregular alleys, the half-block closure of 24th Street between avenues N½ and O, perhaps created by the railroad that once ran down Avenue N, creates an often overlooked area. Several historic homes are scattered among more recent constructions.

1503–05 24th Street

This Queen Anne duplex was built in 1900, while the house next door, 15 years later. Also built that year was the duplex at **1511** which was originally a single-family dwelling.

1607 24th Street

This Prairie style brick house was built in 1927, with its garden running alongside. Note the detail in the fish scale siding of the tiny 1908 cottage next door. At the dead end is another small cottage that was built in 1906.

▶ 7 Retrace your steps to Avenue N½ and turn right. Walk east on the south side of the street.

Back along Avenue N½, you'll find a 1927 Colonial Revival at **2327**, next to a 1915 bungalow. Across the street at **2324 Avenue N½** stands a cottage built in 1892.

▶ 8 Turn right and walk south to Avenue O.

Before the Civil War, 23rd (aka Tremont) was the most prestigious street in the city. Unfortunately, most of those impressive residences, including W. L. Moody Jr.'s first home, gave way to commercial development. Galveston architect, Clarence E. Stevens, designed the Elks Club, B.P.O.E. #126, in the middle of the block at **1518 23rd Street** in 1950 to replace a magnificent building on Postoffice Street, between 21st and 22nd Streets. Across 23rd St., you'll see two similar homes at **1604** and **1606**. Insurance records note that they were built around 1903. Hurricane Carla in 1961 spawned a tornado which bounced down 23rd Street before veering east to 21st Street, explaining the more modern construction.

▶ ❾ Turn right on Avenue O, walking west on the north side of the street.

2323 Avenue O

You'll find several old homes among the newer, some as recent as 1970. Looking across the street you'll see the stuccoed Henry Trueheart Adriance Mediterranean home, built in 1924. Now a Bed and Breakfast, note the side porch to the east and the porte cache on the west side, with an apparent garage apartment in the back. Next door on the corner stands a Classic Revival with its rounded double verandas built in 1910.

On this side of Avenue O, you'll pass several Queen Anne designs at **2318**, **2320** and **2324**, all built in 1900.

2328 Avenue O

Plasterer John M. Rourke built this Queen Anne design with ample gingerbread on its projecting double verandas in 1886. **2404-08** is a triplex built in 1941.

2412 Avenue O

This brick Prairie style house was built in 1934 for "rough spoken" gambling don, Rosario Maceo. Note its green tiled roof.

▶ Back at your car, this concludes your Silk Stocking Stroll.

19th St.
4
21st St.
22nd St.
23rd St.
24th St.
Avenue P
Avenue Q
1
2
3
25th St.
26th St.
Seawall Blvd.
27th St.
5

CHAPTER 5

Seawall Excursion

▶ ❶ Park your car at 25th Street and Avenue Q½—the first street behind Seawall Boulevard. You'll pass several eateries on your walk so consider stopping for a snack, either before, during, or after your exploration.

▶ ❷ Turn left, walking south toward the Gulf of Mexico, crossing the Boulevard at the light.

▶ ❸ Turn left, walking east on the Seawall proper.

Galveston's Seawall was a direct result of the 1900 Storm, which changed the Island's destiny forever. On the first anniversary of the hurricane, city fathers pledged to protect the Island city from future hurricanes by first building a concrete bulwark spanning the Gulf, then raising the elevation of the city above sea level.

Legend has it that Col. H. M. Robert with the U.S. Corps of Engineers designed and had proposed this bulwark against the sea just one week before the 1900 Storm. Actually, Henry

Galveston's Seawall dimensions
—Courtesy of The Rosenberg Library, Galveston, Texas

Martyn chaired a board of three consulting engineers whose collective recommendations were incorporated in its design. With its Gulf side concaved, the Seawall stands sixteen feet tall—that's how high the water rose during the 1900 Storm—sixteen feet wide at its base and five feet wide on top. It was completed in sections, moving east to west, using a moveable mold. Except for those funded by the U. S. government to protect their military installations, Galveston County completed the rest of the Seawall, including the 500 foot rock groins added in 1936 to prevent sand from washing out from beneath the bulwark. The final section, from 61st to 102nd streets, was completed in 1963, making the Seawall a total of 10.4 miles long, which is only one-third of the Island's total length. According to Guinness, Galveston's Seawall holds the World's Record for the Longest Continuous Sidewalk. By the way, after a promotion just before he retired in 1901, this celebrated Brigadier General also wrote *Robert's Rules of Order* outlining parliamentary procedures.

23rd and Seawall Boulevard

This granite monument marks the completion of the first part of the Seawall in 1904.

The second part of the city's ambitious plan to protect the Island from nature was to raise the grade of the city above sea level. Local government contracted with the German firm of Messrs. Goedhart and Bates who supplied four specially-built dredges from Holland. Working 24/7 from December 12, 1905, through August 27, 1911, they deepened the entrance to the port. Then, the dredges pumped the stinky sludge into the east end by means of a canal along the new Seawall. When the liquefied sand dried, Galveston stood an average of eight feet taller. Their two-part plan proved itself when a stronger storm struck the Island in 1915 with a tidal surge of 21 feet. Only 12 deaths were reported in the east end.

Over the Gulf of Mexico at 21st Street once stood the Balinese Room, infamous showplace of "The Free State of Galveston." Unfortunately, Hurricane Ike demolished the building, leaving only memories behind.

The Balinese Room
—Courtesy of the Texas Historical Commission

2107 Seawall

While the Island recovered from the 1900 Storm, Houston financially dethroned the "Queen City of the Gulf" with its new oil industry. In 1915, the ship channel opened. Many of the large ships you see on the horizon are actually on their way to Houston. The once-decadent city of Galveston had to find other means of economic development.

Sicilian-born brothers named Maceo—the affable Sam and his rougher-spoken sibling, Rosario ("Rose")—began their Island career as barbers. By the time Prohibition started April 1918, they had drifted into bootlegging. This was merely the beginning of their illegal empire. When the stock market crashed on October 29, 1929, the brothers had cornered the market on gambling too.

In partnership with two "gangs," they opened the ritzy Hollywood Dinner Club at 61st and Stewart in 1926—the first air-conditioned supper club to offer top-name entertainment, drinking, dining and dancing—with a little illegal gambling in its private back room. Famous entertainers, such as Guy Lombardo and his Royal Canadians, Glenn Miller, the Ritz Brothers, Sophie Tucker, Edgar Bergen with Charlie McCarthy, Phil Harris, Frank Sinatra, Peggy Lee and Jimmy Dorsey found their way to Galveston Island via the Maceos over the next thirty years.

Here over the sand, Sam and Rose owned the small Grotto, which became a Chinese restaurant in 1932 called the Sui Jen (pronounced Swee Rin). After local authorities closed the Hollywood, the restaurant was remodeled into another swanky supper club and renamed the Balinese Room, more politically correct one month after Pearl Harbor.

Adding a 500 foot pier that stretched out over the Gulf, with a T-head at its end to accommodate the private back room, the Maceo brothers moved their Hollywood operations to 2107 Seawall, inviting Houston's oil-rich "High Rollers" to "Come Down and Play on Galveston Island."

And play they did—until Attorney General Will Wilson pledged to "close down Galveston" using the Texas Rangers. Regular raids became routine, and sometimes part of the show, but by the time the lawmen reached the back room at the end of "Rangers Run," no evidence of illegal gambling could be found. Then, an inside informant gave them a plan of action. On June 5, 1957, several Rangers took a boat under the T-head and stationed themselves strategically at the windows of the private gambling room. As usual, when the doorman saw the obvious 10-gallon-white hats of the Texas Rangers running down the Seawall, he pressed a buzzer that sounded in the club, signaling the band to play, "The Eyes of Texas Are Upon You." Those at the windows watched as slot machines disappeared into the walls like Murphy beds. Money seemed to drop through the floor as crap and poker tables were converted into backgammon and bridge within two minutes, before the fastest Ranger arrived. With that, all future illegal bets were off.

▶ ④ Cross Seawall Boulevard at 19th Street Turn left, walking back west.

Looking a block east, you'll note the only private residence left on the Seawall at 18th Street. Surrounded by a tall white wall, the clean, classic 1913 design was home to shipping agent, Fred A. Langbehn. It survived the 1915 Storm with only minor damage due to its deep pile foundations and concrete construction, according to the owner.

2024 Seawall Boulevard

The impressive Hotel Galvez dominates two blocks on the Seawall between 19th and 21st streets. Built by Galveston businessmen in 1911, this million dollar monument symbolized the Island would return as a premier beach resort. D. W. Kempner, who led the group, hired the architectural firm of Mauran, Russell and Garden of St. Louis, who had designed his home on Avenue O at Rosenberg (see the Silk Stocking Stroll.) Recessed behind an expansive lawn, this six-story Spanish

Hotel Galvez

—From author's collection of postcards

Colonial Revival structure boasted 250 rooms on the "European plan."

The investors named their luxury hotel after Count Bernardo de Galvez, for whom "Galvez Town" was named. This Spanish viceroy had commissioned a survey of the Island in 1784, but died of Yellow Fever in New Orleans before it was completed. Ironically, the motto on his coat of arms read, "Yo Solo" or "I Alone," which characterizes the independent spirit of Galvestonians.

Over the years, the Hotel Galvez served many. As the center of social life, its ballroom witnessed the debuts of many young women. President Franklin D. Roosevelt commandeered the hotel as the southern White House during a fishing trip in 1937. During World War II, the U. S. Coast Guard drafted the Galvez as their headquarters for two years. Balinese Room gambling don Sam Maceo, once a barber here, lived in the penthouse suite. Popular entertainer Phil Harris borrowed his apartment in 1941 to marry Alice Faye in a quiet ceremony, because the bride was unsure their Tijuana vows were legal. One eyewitness account at the ceremony—a little girl named Betty Jo —remembered the bride's flawless complexion mirrored by an abundance of pink. Speaking of brides, legend has it that a restless little spirit wanders the fifth floor in search of her seafaring fiancé.

Walk through the impressive lobby, aka the sun parlor or loggia, of the Hotel Galvez to feel its past grandeur. At its entry are historical displays. Notice the black and white, wall-sized photographs which were taken during its grand opening on June 10, 1911. Among them is a photo of swimmers in the Crystal Palace Gulf-fed pool which once stood on the west corner of 23rd and Seawall Boulevard. This well-rounded amusement center offered a restaurant, dance pavilion, a penny arcade, gambling and an indoor saltwater swimming pool. The portrait on the west wall outside the ballroom, now called the Music Room, is of Count Bernardo himself.

Serving its original protective purpose, Galveston's Seawall was never intended as a traditional residential neighborhood. Instead, investors valued its location for commercial tourism development on Galveston Island—even before it was built!

Crystal Palace

—From author's personal collection

In 1881, Nicholas Clayton designed the Galveston Pavilion at 21st Street to house the annual Saengerfest, a convention of German men's chorales. This ornate bathhouse, the first building in Texas with electric lighting, burned down just two years later. Briefly adjoining it was the Beach Hotel. Built on the sand beneath the intersection of 23rd and Seawall Boulevard, this three-story Queen Anne featured wide, multi-leveled verandas and a central octagonal dome. It too burned, under mysterious circumstances, in 1898.

Just imagine what these two blocks of beachfront must have looked like in the past, with their various visitor amusements.

At 25th Street, a 60 foot sign proclaimed, "Galveston: The Treasure Island of America." This was a gift to the city from Brush Electric in September 1912. A later amusement, the Electric Park, dominated 23rd just off the Seawall until the 1915 Storm leveled both.

With pennants flying, The Breakers and The Surf Bath House at 33rd Street offered a variety of amusements, befitting the "Atlantic City of the South." In fact, the Seawall could have been a model for the future Las Vegas Strip with its bathhouses, dance pavilions and supper clubs—all equipped with Maceo "slots" during its "Free State" era.

Electric Park

—From the author's personal collection

The Breakers

—From the author's personal collection

To rival the Hotel Galvez, W. L. Moody, Jr., built his Buccaneer Hotel on a triangular lot on the east side of 23rd and Seawall in 1929. Labeled as Spanish Renaissance in design with Hispano-Moorish features, the 11-story building boasted 440 rooms and spectacular aerial views of the city, including the wooden Mountain Speedway (aka "The Wild Mouse" in later years) rollercoaster behind the hotel. In 1963, Cameron Fairchild converted the hotel into apartments for the elderly, called Edgewater Methodist Retirement Community. When the high rise became impractical and unsafe for seniors—and insurance and restoration costs too prohibitive—the Buccaneer was imploded on January 1, 1999, replaced by new construction that fronts 23rd Street. Next door to the east, the Moodys built a Civic Center in 1957, which asbestos brought down in May 2005.

On the Gulf side, only remnants remain of the original Murdoch's Pier, another victim of Ike.

2501 Seawall Boulevard

Although battered by Hurricane Ike, the structure over the Gulf at the foot of Rosenberg holds the promise to unite past, present and future on Galveston Island.

The idea of a Municipal Pleasure Pier originated as early 1912. After all, Atlantic City had her Boardwalk! However, plans for a 700 foot pier and auditorium were not drawn until 1931 by R. R. Rapp. Construction stopped on the city project during World War II, when it was requisitioned by both Army and Navy for storage. When finally completed in 1944, the Pleasure Pier measured 1,130 feet and included a ballroom for dancing to the Big Band sound, an aquarium, a 2,000-seat outdoor theatre, restaurants and a snack bar, with a T-head fishing pier on the Gulf end. The Maceos and W. L. Moody, Jr., air conditioned it four years later. That next February, knot-headed Mardi Gras King, Charlie McCarthy with his voice, Edgar Bergen, welcomed 1,300 to celebrate on the already-outdated Pleasure Pier. After Hurricane Carla leveled the amusements in 1961, the city leased the pier to James E. Lyon of Houston. Governmental financial finagling funded the Flagship Hotel in 1965, the first built over water in the United States. Today, Houston entrepreneur, Tilman Fertitta—the Island's latest mover-and-shaker—plans to restore the hotel and pier into a turn-of-the-century Boardwalk, completing the Atlantic City circle.

▶Continue walking west, crossing 25th Street.

▶Cross 27th Street.

27th–29th Streets on the Seawall

In her book *Island of Color*, Izola Collins remembers that African American businessman Robert Maguire once owned this two-block area of the beachfront, complete with private bathhouse. It was traditionally reserved for "people of color," sometimes crudely referred to as the "black beach." Maguire had financed his investment with his hack stand downtown, offering his horse and buggy for hire. His two blocks became an entertainment venue for the black community, hosting many Juneteenth celebrations. Collins states that the "land was later taken from them," after the grade raising. Tax records indicate that the Galveston Commercial Association owned it until 1914, when they sold it to the City of Galveston. Menard Park and Playground was developed, complete with tennis courts on Avenue Q and a bandstand on its beach side, which was replaced in 1950 by a "modern bandshell" designed by Raymond Rapp. A World War II USO building fronted 27th Street next to the tennis courts, but was demolished several years ago after its roof caved in. The park and playground was redesigned in 2008 to include a skate park. The new McGuire-Dent Recreation Center, scheduled to open early next year, stands near the Seawall and stretches across its south side behind the 1950's bandshell.

Two monuments face Seawall Boulevard. A granite bench, centered within the two-block area, salutes Galveston World War I casualties, including those "colored." To its east stands another monument erected by the Texas Society of the Daughters of American Colonists in 1937, commemorating the Texas Navy which, "played a heroic part of the Texas Republic and made their headquarters at the port of Galveston."

▶❺ Turn right to retrace your steps back to 25th Street. Turn left to find your car.

▶To finish your Seawall Excursion, drive west along the Gulf of Mexico to 53rd Street. This is a driving tour on your way to your next walk and is reflected on that map.

The Surf Hotel at 33rd Street and Seawall
—From the author's personal collection

Ft. Crockett

From 39th to 53rd Streets, the Federal government funded the Seawall project in 1905 to protect its Fort Crockett. Established in 1897 for coastal defense, this 125-acre Army installation provided artillery training using three gun emplacements. It served as a mobilization center during the Mexican border war in 1912. The U.S. Army erected permanent barracks just in time for World War I. During the Second World War, German prisoners of war were interned here. Now, there is an unofficial neighborhood association named for this army base.

Seawall at 41st Street

As you drive, note the right side of the Seawall, where you'll see housing for non-commissioned officers. The Office of the Quartermaster built these duplexes in 1939, as well as another group on 53rd Street. Although Fort Crockett closed in 1953, some of its early 20th century buildings still stand. You'll pass the Barracks and Post Exchange as well as the enlisted men's barracks, both one block off the Seawall between 53rd and 45th Streets on Avenue U and Fort Crockett Boulevard.

4800 Block on the Seawall side

On September 9, 2000, as a community choir sang the hymn "Queen of the Waves," this monument to the 1900 Storm victims was dedicated during a rainstorm that cut speeches short. Galveston born sculpture, David Moore, designed the piece which depicts a father, with outstretched hand to the heavens, mother and child to symbolize the spirit of ". . . those who perished and the tenacity of those who survived this nation's deadliest natural disaster."

5222 Seawall

George Mitchel's Woodlands Development Corporation built the 15-story San Luis Hotel and adjoining Condominiums in 1984 on Ft. Crockett's World War II gun batteries. Designed by Eugene Aubry, its S-curve plan affords guests excellent views of the Gulf of Mexico, city, and Seawall. Tillman Fertita now owns the Conference Center complex which stretches to 57th Street.

▶Turn right on 53rd St., then another right at the four-way stop on Avenue U.

5001–07 Avenue U

Despite contradictory information, it appears that this building served as Ft. Crockett's Station Dispensary according to a promotional pamphlet published circa 1948. At that time, the fort had been converted into the Galveston Recreation Center for the Fourth Army, featuring the ". . . most popular sports with G. I. vacationists." Citing concern for this building, Gladys Barrileaux of the *Galveston Daily News* verified its use in a story published on June 5, 1968. Originally Spanish Mediterranean in design, it has been remodeled beyond recognition to accommodate various educational entities over the years. Its open-air galleries remain, however. Fertitta Hospitality Corporation, which owns the San Luis, has just bought the building, but no plans have been announced.

▶**Turn right at Sias, then left on Fort Crockett Boulevard.**

4700 Fort Crockett Boulevard

On the north side of the street, you'll pass the Barracks, Post Exchange and gymnasium. Built in 1911, this Spanish Mission style is marked by its arched galleries, central decorative doorway and red tile roof. Note its open-air galleries, designed to catch the Gulf breezes. Behind and partially visible from Avenue U, are the mess and lavatory buildings. The complex now houses the National Marine Fisheries lab.

4502 Fort Crockett Boulevard

Ft. Crockett's original headquarters still stands at the corner of 45th and Avenue U even though its exterior has been extensively altered.

▶**Turn left at 45th Street and left again at Avenue U, ending your driving tour of the Seawall and Ft. Crockett. Your Seawall Excursion, both east and west, is complete.**

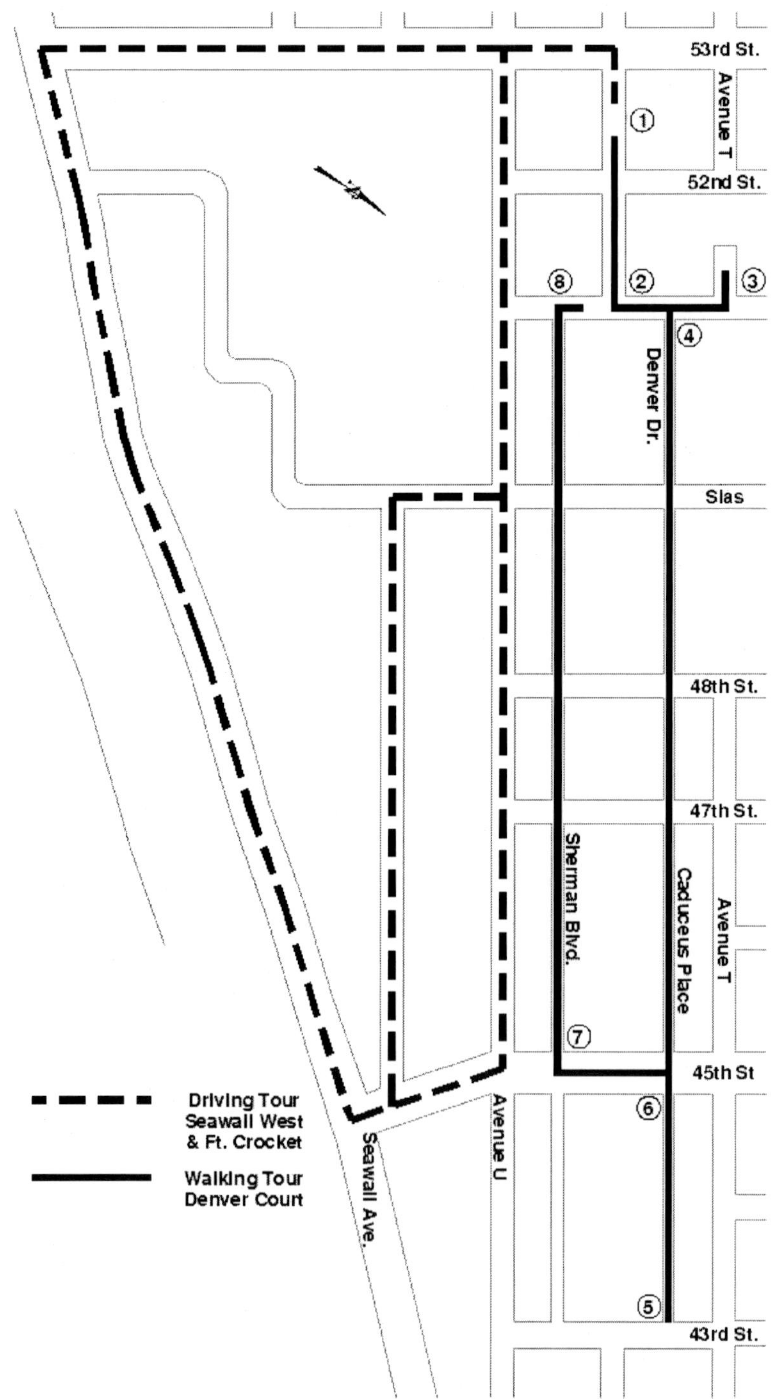
53rd St.
Avenue T
52nd St.
Denver Dr.
Slas
48th St.
47th St.
Sherman Blvd.
Caduceus Place
Avenue T
45th St
Avenue U
Seawall Ave.
43rd St.
Driving Tour
Seawall West
& Ft. Crocket
Walking Tour
Denver Court
1
2
3
4
5
6
7
8

CHAPTER 6

Roarin' Twenties Realms in the Denver Resurvey

▶To begin your next neighborhood walk from the west end of your Seawall Excursion, turn right on 53rd Street. Turn right again on Denver Drive, which is directly aligned with the Moody Memorial Methodist Church.

In 1890, Galveston's H. M. Trueheart and Julius Runge joined with a group of investors from Denver, Colorado, to form the Galveston Land and Improvement Company. They bought 660 acres on the shores of McKinney's Bayou in the southwest third of the original Groesbeck town plan, intended as a middle class housing development. Unfortunately, finances delayed their plan. Then, the 1900 Storm destroyed their low-lying, marshy investment.

Nine years later, the bayou was filled as part of the grade raising. The area was named the Denver Resurvey after the 1890s original. Ripe for development by Galveston's entrepreneurial elite, two subdivisions evolved off 45th Street and south of Broadway that offset the city's Groesbeck grid. You will explore both of these restricted residential subdivisions in two separate walks: Denver Court in this chapter and Cedar Lawn in Chapter 7.

Bordered by the Ft. Crockett installation on its south, the Denver Court Historical District was replatted in 1925 with the automobile in mind, interrupting the Groesbeck grid by a mere ½ block, to discourage traffic and insure the residents' privacy. The neighborhood, however, still adheres to his numbering pattern with even numbered addresses on the north side of the street and odd, on the south.

In 1925, one lawyer and a group of doctors lead by Dr. Willard R. Cooke developed Caduceus Place, naming it in honor of their profession. According to Webster, a caduceus is a "staff with two entwined snakes and two wings at the top . . . symbolizing a physician." The street featured sidewalk-less wide open lawns, long double blocks, larger lots—and race restrictions. For further distinction, a rose hue was added to its concrete street, which dead-ends in oleanders. Despite its semi-brick walled entry on 45th Street, a style that originated in St. Louis, the Place extended west a block after the oleander blockade to another off-set street, Denver Drive.

With demand growing, Brantley Harris, the lawyer in the Caduceus group, further subdivided the property in 1928. In partnership with his brother, Fletcher, they named the entire neighborhood Denver Court; sometimes, it is referred to as Westmoor. Even though the District also includes Woodrow and Crockett, your walk will cover only the oldest streets—Denver Drive, Caduceus Place and Sherman, in that order.

Since none of the houses in this neighborhood has been on the Galveston Historic Foundation's annual Homes Tour, much of their human stories are sketchy, especially on Sherman. But they are certainly worth seeing and wondering about as you wander these streets. Again, please stay on the public thoroughfares.

Enjoy your architectural exploration of Galveston's historic west end.

▶ ❶ Park your car near your first house, 5209 Denver Drive and walk east.

5209 Denver Drive

Architect and developer, Ben J. Kotin designed this house for his family in 1958. Both he and his partner, Tibor Beerman, used brick screens as their trademark, this one enclosing the entrance.

Note how the entrance to the cathedral-like Moody Memorial Methodist Church at **2803 53rd Street** is purposely centered with the street as part of the 1964 design by Dallas architect Mark Lemmon. The tall brick wall and heavy vegetation on the left conceals another Moody home, captioned after your first turn.

5127 Denver Drive

Ben Milam designed this Georgian/Regency composite for Ernest A. Rees, an ANICO official, in 1940. The sloping wall to the west hides the driveway and garage. Also note the 1951 split level home at **5115** as well the 1941 modern house at **5109**.

5101 Denver Drive

This house began as a 1930s Federal style, but has been extended southward over the years. You'll see that new addition toward the end of your walk.

▶ ❷ Turn left on 51st Street and walk ½ a block. At the Avenue T street sign, turn to the left again. Although it appears to be private property, it is a public thoroughfare—talk about off-set!

5115 Avenue T

Through the gates to the left, note the red brick country manor. Designed by John Staub in 1938, this house was built for W. L. Moody, III, and his wife, Mary Margaret Guinard. Rather plain by design, it features tall floor to ceiling shuttered windows. As noted in the *Galveston Architectural Guide* (Moody) "succeeded in building the biggest house in the neighborhood, even if it is practically invisible."

5128 Avenue T

Its neighbor to the right, behind its own gate that overlooks a fountain, was built two years later for Moody's daughter Edna and her husband, David B. T. Myrick, an executive with

American National Insurance Company. A later owner, Giosue "Sonny" Martini, added an angled wing to hold his private movie screening room. After all, he owned the Martini and State (aka the restored Grand 1894 Opera House) Theatres located near 21st and Postoffice streets in downtown Galveston.

▶ ❸ **Retrace your steps back to Denver Drive on 51st Street.**

▶ ❹ **Turn left, walking east.**

This block contains many Colonial Revival designs on both sides of the street: **5016** (1937), **5017** (1939), **5113** (1942) and **5011** (1941). In contrast, **5005** is Monterey style, built in 1955.

5012 Denver Drive

Julian A. Levy, of the E. S. Levy clothing store, built this elegant Georgian house in 1947. Designed by Raymond Rapp, the elaborate entry features cast stone centered on a portico of white wood columns. Fanny Kempner Adoue lived here later.

In the next part of the block, only two houses are of particular note, both on the south side of the street: **4905 Denver**, a Colonial Revival from 1939, and **4901** which was built six years earlier in the Italian Renaissance style.

▶ **Cross Sias.**

4813 Denver Drive

This quaint Tudor Revival manor house was designed by Cameron Fairchild in 1930 for W. Kendall Menard, while its Colonial Revival neighbor was built six years later.

4811 Denver Drive

The style of this 1929 home incorporates Tudor with Prairie.

4810 Denver Drive

Houston architect Irving Klein designed this Regency villa in 1940 for Marvin Kahn who managed Nathan's Clothing store on Postoffice just off 23rd Street. However, Ruth Kempner (and husband Harris, who died at age 84 in 1987 while playing tennis) lived here from 1946 to 1991.

4805 Denver

Built in 1929, this French Eclectic stands next to a Modern design from 1951.

4806 Denver Drive

The 1941 Julian Ormond home across the street, designed by Raymond Rapp, is a miniature version of the Levy house.

▶Cross 48th Street. Note that Denver Drive becomes Caduceus Place.

4727 Denver

This Neo Classical was built in 1933, while its neighbor is another 1950s Modern home. Across the street stands a Tudor Revival built five years later.

4720 Caduceus

Note the curvature of the entry portico of this two story red brick Colonial Revival that was built in 1937.

4715 Caduceus

This 1929 Tudor Revival contrasts sharply with the Colonial Revival built four years later next door. Note the 1938 French Eclectic at **4708 Caduceus** across the street and the 1928 Prairie style next door.

▶Cross 47th Street and walk through the oleander bush blockade of Caduceus Place.

This street was the first street developed in the Denver Court Historic District. No numbered street intersects the next two blocks of extra-large lots and rose tinted concrete pavement.

4626 Caduceus Place

Monterey in style, this 1938 Louis Pauls House was designed by Cameron Fairchild.

4625 Caduceus Place

Across the street stands a 1937 Ben Milam Tudor Revival built for Dr. George W. N. Eggers.

4615 Caduceus Place

Built in 1941 for Leland S. Dennis, vice president of the Cotton Concentration Company, this handsome home features an elliptical portico. Designed by Harvin Moore and Herman Lloyd, the stark whiteness of this Neo Classical style accents its simplicity.

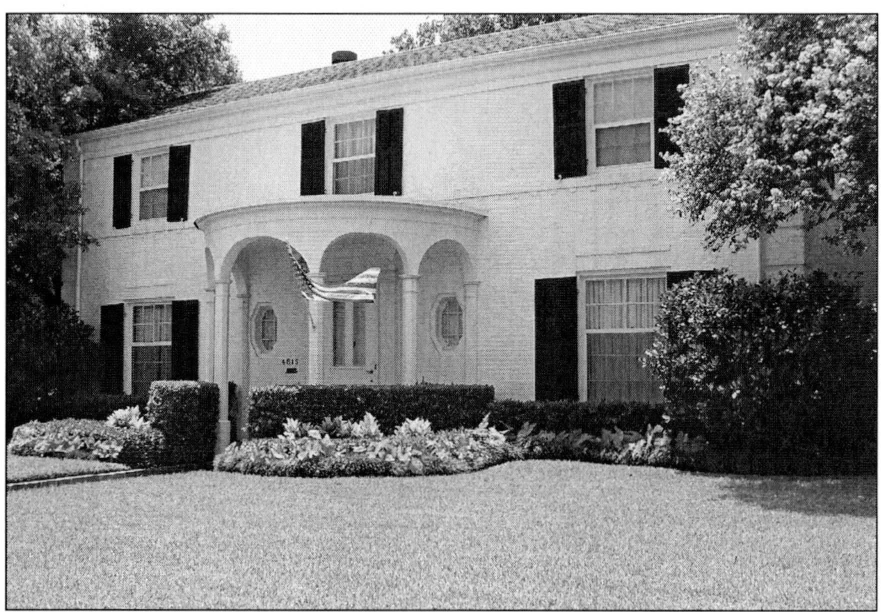

The Leland S. Dennis House

4603 Caduceus Place

Note the metal screen which hides floor to ceiling windows, designed by Thomas Price in 1956. In contrast, the traditional Colonial Revival across the street was built in 1937 for Dr. George T. Lee.

4525 Caduceus Place

Cameron Fairchild based the style of this 1930 Spanish Mediterranean house on a house in Houston that was designed by Harrie T. Lindeberg of New York. John W. McCullough, an executive of various George Sealy interests, built the house for his wife, a Menard-Sherman-Trueheart descendant. Moving here in 1962, architect Thomas Price lived here for ten years.

4520 Caduceus Place

Galveston's mayor in 1939 and one of the developers of the Denver Court neighborhood, Brantly Harris built this bungalow in 1926. Originally designed by Raymond Rapp, Cameron Fairchild contributed additions to the lawyer's Neo Classical in 1938. Note its dormers, front door and the guest quarters on the property.

4510 Caduceus Place

The first house built in Denver Court was this Craftsman style, with a Neo Classic influence in its dormers and front porch. Designed by Stowe and Stowe for Dr. Willard R. Cooke, an ob-gyn professor at UTMB and second developer of the district, built the simple, stucco home in 1926. The west wing is not original.

Dr. Willard R. Cooke Home at entry to Caduceus Place

4505 Caduceus Place

Lawyer Bryan Williams hired San Antonio architects, Phelps and Dewees, to design his country house in 1932. While this is their only house on Galveston Island, this firm designed many of the revival style country homes in the San Antonio area. Note its slate roof, leaded glass and prominent chimneys. Strategically placed at the entrance to Caduceus Place, this Tudor Revival marks the exclusive enclave with manor-like style.

▶ Cross 45th St.—cautiously, as this is a very busy thoroughfare!

You'll view the homes on the north side of the street first.

4428 Caduceus

Miss Lillian Schadt built the two-story Italian villa for her mother, Mrs. William Schadt, in 1930. Faced with stucco, the Moorish influence in its arched doors and brackets enhance its Mediterranean feel.

4420 Cacudeus Place

In contrast, Dr. and Mrs. Menelaus Caravageli built their Contemporary home in 1953. Typical of the style at the time is the glass gable below the slightly peaked but mostly flat roof.

4402 Caduceus Place

Houston architect, Bailey Swenson, brought the Riverside Terrace

The Victor Reiswerg House

area of that city to Galveston in this Contemporary Ranch in 1951. Outstanding in Victor Reiswerg's home is his mother-in-law's room—centered and the only room on the second floor.

▶ ❺ Cross the street and turn right, walking back west on the south side.

4313 Caduceus Place

Another Houston architect and Rice graduate, Harvin C. Moore designed this house in 1946 for the Methodist pastor of what would become the Moody Memorial Methodist Church in 1964. Based on the Alsatian architecture of Castroville, Texas, this home features a stone veneer—very rare in Galveston.

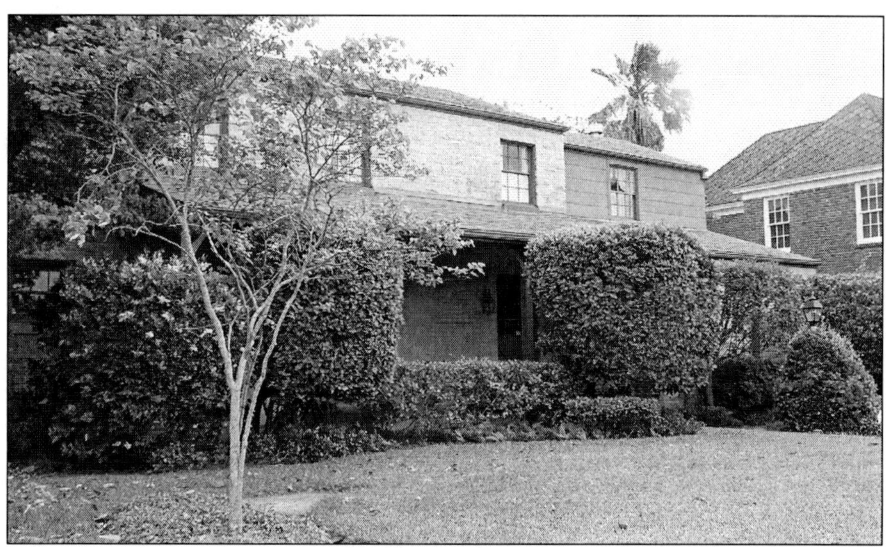

4313 Caduceus Place

4319 Caduceus Place

The conservative 1948 Monterey house of the Miles K. Burton family was designed by Charles I. Zwiener.

4321 Caduceus Place

This 1936 multi-cubed Modern was built by Robert I. Cohen, III, of the family's clothing store by the same name. Also called

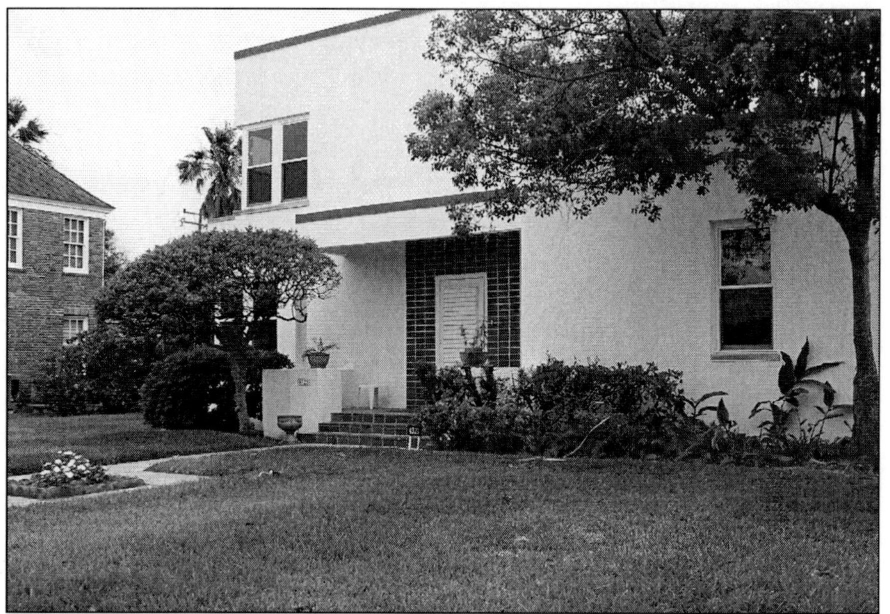

Robert I. Cohen's multi-cubed Modern

the International style, note its glass-block windows at the corners of the cubes—an Art Deco touch. The sidewalk continues this interlock pattern of the white stucco cubes of the house.

▶ 6 Cross 45th Street again and walk one block south to Sherman Boulevard.

▶ 7 Turn right, walking west.

Please remember that many of the human stories have never been told. However, the basic architectural data of the houses you'll pass has been listed.

The two Tudor Revival houses on the right corners were built twelve years apart: **4427 Sherman Boulevard** in 1929 and **4428** on the north corner in 1941.

Except for the Modern 1948 design at **4501 Sherman**, the next two blocks of Sherman feature homes built during the late 1920s. Note, too, that **4528** is very new construction.

4515 Sherman Boulevard

Most notable is this Spanish Eclectic. Note the U-shaped driveway, front courtyard and red clay tile roof of this 1927 design.

4603 Sherman

Like its neighbor, this is a Modern design. Restaurateur Nick M. Cokins hired Thomas Price to design his courtyard house in 1956.

4602 Sherman Boulevard

Galveston architect Raymond Rapp designed the Neo Classic house of Joseph J. Kane of the Kane Boiler Works in 1927. The neighborhood was new, but this stately home reflects an old-fashioned conservatism.

The rest of the 4600 block includes another Neo Classic built in 1927, **4628**; a French Eclectic at **4625** from 1939; two Tudor Revivals at **4611** and **4620**, both built in 1935 and, at **4615**, a 1929 Colonial Revival.

▶ **Cross 47th Street.**

The further west you walk on Sherman, the more varied the houses. The historic homes in the next block of Sherman Boulevard were constructed from 1929 to 1939 in varying popular designs of that decade—Tudor Revival (**4701** and **4715**), Tudor (**4702**), Craftsman (**4720**) and Neo Classic (**4727**).

▶ **Cross 48th Street.**

This block contains another eclectic mix of styles, from those built in 1929—the Colonial Revival at **4804**, a Modern at **4805**, and a Tudor Revival at **4809** to a 1952 Ranch at **4801 Sherman** and a 1937 Colonial Revival next door. Three other Colonial Revivals from the 1940s are seen at **4815**, **4817**, and **4818**. A 1931 Modern design stands at **4816**.

4820 Sherman Boulevard

Built in 1938, this one-story Tudor Revival cottage features a

4820 Sherman Blvd.

round tower with pyramid-shaped roof at its entrance. Also note its large red brick chimney.

▶ Cross Sias. Note that the 4900 numbers are missing.

The houses in the 5000 block of Sherman Boulevard were built between the Tudor Revival in 1936 at **5003** and the 1951 Ranch style at **5015**.

5007 Sherman

Note the two-car garage of the 1948 Modern design—unusual for that time.

5006 and 5010 Sherman.

These two homes were both built in 1948 and considered in the Minimal Traditional.

5012 Sherman Boulevard

One of the first modern houses in the Denver Court area was designed by architect Charles Zwiener for his own family in 1949. He also designed the Contemporary home next door to the west in 1950 for Dr. and Mrs. Y. C. Smith, Jr.

5017 Sherman Boulevard

This Colonial Revival, also designed by Zwiener, was built in 1951 for the McDonald family. The Colonial Revival next door was built in 1940.

5020 Sherman

A unique design for this street is this 1945 French Eclectic home.

▶ ❽ Turn right and walk the half block back to Denver Dr., to find your car.

Note the new addition to **5101**.

You've completed your first walk in the Roarin' Twenties Realm of the Denver Court Historic District.

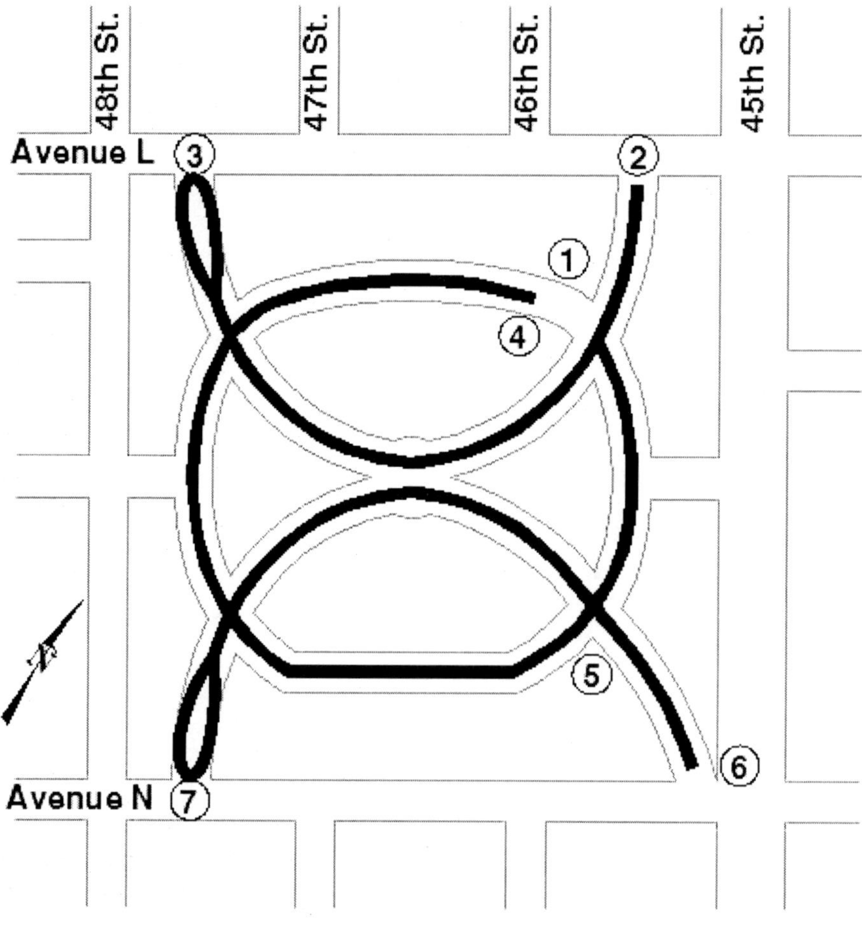
48th St.
47th St.
46th St.
45th St.
Avenue L
Avenue N
1
2
3
4
5
6
7

CHAPTER 7

Cedar Lawn–Against the Grid

In 1926, Clark W. Thompson joined with his brother-in-law, W. L. Moody, III, and Moody's father in law, W. D. Haden, to establish the first fully planned residential community on Galveston Island. Intended as an enclave for the Moody family and company men, Cedar Lawn followed a "butterfly" pattern within nine square blocks that turned "its back to the city" (or so it seemed to Beasley and Fox). Legend has it that this maze-like configuration originated in Baltimore, Maryland, in the late 19th century. By the 1920s, it had been popularized in the southwest. Basically, it consists of one large circle intersected by two half circles that meet in the middle to form a round central garden. It is a one-of-a-kind configuration in the state of Texas.

To further preserve the integrity of "Galveston's Garden Spot," strict deed restrictions included a minimum cost per home, setback rules with no sidewalks allowed, narrow winding streets (which prohibit motor coaches) graded to drain down the middle, liquor prohibition—and race restrictions.

Thompson, a twenty-year veteran in the U.S. House of Representatives, built the first house at #15 North Drive, while Moody completed his large red brick compound across the central garden within five years. During the late 1940s, gambling don Sam Maceo moved in his men, building his own home in this "isolated, homogenous pocket of the elite" (so called by Texas Historical Commission) in 1950.

After their exclusive neighborhood was underway, the Cedar Lawn Development Company bought eight blocks to its west, between 45th and 48th Streets, avenues L and N ½. Named Palm Gardens, its slightly off-set streets were named after Texas heroes. Meant for more middle-class housing, Palm Gardens remains an overlooked neighborhood in the local preservation scheme of things.

Completely gated in 1998, Cedar Lawn forms a distinct community that features tall, brick walled fences and an abundance of flora. This District remains the best preserved and most cohesive residential neighborhood on the Island.

But its butterfly pattern can be tricky! This guide is routed for you to walk the North Drive (a half circle) first, even though you'll have to retrace your steps. Finding yourself back at your parked car, you'll then walk the longest street, the elliptical Cedar Lawn Circle. To avoid confusion, drive your car around the Circle to the South Drive (although it's certainly within walking distance) to complete your exploration of Cedar Lawn. Try not to veer off these paths until you finish each one as it can get very confusing in this maze!

▶Going north on 53rd Street, turn right on Broadway to 45th Street. Turn right. Two blocks south of Broadway, you'll find the prestigious Cedar Lawn Historical District, marked by a small brick entry. Turn right off 45th Street into the neighborhood.

▶❶ Turn right and park on Cedar Lawn Circle alongside the wood fenced back yard of #5 North, just past where North Drive intersects the Circle. Walking, turn left from your parked car to find the beginning of North Drive.

#5 North Drive

Vice President of American National Insurance Company, William J. Shaw, hired architect Donald MacKenzie in 1929 to design his two-story Italianate house. Maceo family accountant,

Sam "Books" Serio bought this home in 1952 and made many changes to its original design.

#4 North Drive

Across the street stands the 1930 John and Pearl Gill Home, a two-story Tudor Revival. Although John's mother—granddaughter of Samuel May Williams—was thoroughly rooted in the city's beginnings, the couple lived here for only one year, when his career moved them to Washington, D.C. The house changed hands several times before the Galveston-Houston Catholic Diocese bought it in 1965 to serve as the rectory for five priests at Our Lady of Guadelupe Catholic Church across 45th Street. When the Diocese discontinued services in 1993, they sold the rectory.

#2 North Drive

Next door, a 1956 Ranch style home, built by Model Dairy owner, David P. Ritter, Sr., has just been modernized.

#1 North Drive

Across the street stands an English Tudor built in 1929 for the Barden family. Note the Bacchus face above entry, which is not original.

▶❷ Retrace your steps when you reach the fence. Continue walking straight on the North Drive, passing #63 on the Circle. Please resist the temptation to turn right onto Cedar Lawn Circle; just cross it. You will pass #1 on the Circle on your left.

#7 North Drive

While **#6 North** across the street is a 1956 contemporary built for William W. McManus, this two-story house, with its unique patterned stucco and green tiled roof, was constructed in 1928. Ray Rolan, secretary and merchandising manager for Clark W. Thompson's mercantile firm, hired R. W. Boney to design his Spanish Eclectic home. After the company went out of business in 1932, he and his wife moved to California. One year later, his widow sold the house to Thomas F. and Cecilia Shaw, who lived here until 1968.

#12 North Drive

With its walled side yard, this house was built in 1927 by Grady Dickinson, who co-owned the Star Drug Store on 23rd Street in downtown Galveston. Twelve years later, Fred Pabst bought the Prairie Mission style. A respected community leader, Pabst served as Chairman of the Seawall Committee for eight years. While County Commissioner, President Woodrow Wilson appointed Pabst Collector of Customs for District 22, which he held for five terms.

#11 North Drive

Dr. Charles T. Stone, UTMB professor of internal medicine, constructed this 1929 stately Georgian home, designed by Raymond Rapp. Note its abundant red brick, elegant entry portico and carriage house. Over the years, only UTMB doctors owned this home.

▶Continuing on North, veer to the right after the circular garden on the left.

#15 North Drive

In 1927 Donald N. McKenzie designed this two-story Tudor Revival for Clark W. Thompson and his wife, Libby—daughter of W. L. Moody, Jr. Simple and unpretentious, its angled Arts-

#15 North Drive

and-Crafts "butterfly" plan maximizes sunlight and southern breezes. In front stands the "Moody Oak."

#17 North Drive

Next door is a 1931 Mediterranean, built by Duncan and Estella McLeod of the Gulf, Colorado and Santa Fe Railroad.

▶Cross Cedar Lawn Circle but continue walking on the North Drive.

#22 North Drive

#22 North Drive

The stately Herman E. Kleinecke home stands to the right of where the Circle intersects the Drive. Built in 1939 for the City Attorney, this white Classical Revival features a grand entry, complete with four Doric columns, curving stairway inside, and a sunroom off the living room. The house next door at **#20** is new construction, built on the original tennis courts of the Kleinecke house.

#21 North Drive

Across the street, a Maceo associate named Joe Glorioso (according to several sources that really was his name) built his "honeymoon house" in 1956 with bricks left over from Sam's home at **#43** on the Circle. The house next door is a contemporary design from 1957, built for W. A. MacKenize.

#24 North

Across the street stands an English Tudor built for J. W. Woodruff in 1928.

➌ Retrace your steps on North Drive back to your car.

Note the tall brick wall and barely perceptible entry to your right. This hides the back entry of the Sam Maceo home which fronts both North Drive and the Circle. You'll read about it when you walk Cedar Lawn Circle.

#84 and **#16 South** on the other side of the circular park are listed on your last walk in the neighborhood. Note the entry to **#12 North** while walking back to your car parked at the intersection of North Drive and Cedar Lawn Circle.

➍ After you reach your car, walk Cedar Lawn Circle by veering to the right.

#63 Cedar Lawn Circle

The grand English Tudor was built in 1927 by Dr. William Gammon, a general practitioner at UTMB.

#66 Cedar Lawn Circle

Across the street, Waples Lumber Company constructed this house in 1929 as an investment. Grocer C. P. Evans lived here until 1933 when he built his own Cedar Lawn home near the entrance at **#8 North**. The house passed to many owners until Geoffrey Miller purchased it during the 1980s and sold it to his parents, Ray and Veronica. This Miller, a former news director, hosted the *Eyes of Texas* on KPRC—Channel 2 and authored many Texas travel guides, including one about Galveston.

#64 Cedar Lawn Circle

This Mediterranean home was also built as an investment in 1930, which H. Gale Rogers bought for his family soon after completion. The two-story features a balcony enclosed by wrought iron over the entry and both a red tile and flat roofs.

#57 Cedar Lawn Circle

Across the street stands a stately red brick Neo-classical home built in 1928 by Thomas W. Lain who established the first trust department in Galveston at the First Hutchings Sealy National

Bank. The house next door at **#53** is new construction from 1966.

#58 Cedar Lawn Circle

While the house next door at **#60** was built in 1954 on its tennis court for Ben and Rebecca Druss, Woodrow J. Walker constructed this modern Mexican Ranchero in 1946. "Woody" and his wife owned the Pier Club and managed the Palace Club for the Maceos. His father-in-law, Mr. Chancey, played with textures and geometry to create an eclectic and whimsical design.

#58 Cedar Lawn Circle

#56 on the Circle

This home reflects an older Prairie/Mission style of 1930.

#50 Cedar Lawn Circle

Wholesale green grocer Jack Demack, Jr., built the sprawling one-story Ranch in 1956. Demack Produce had been in business on The Strand over 120 years when it closed in 1987. Built closer to the street than the original Cedar Lawn Deed Restrictions would allow, the new house next door replaced an original 1926 house in 1987.

▶ **Cross North Drive, continuing on the Circle. The brick wall on your right encloses the garden of #21 North.**

#44 Cedar Lawn Circle

Next to a Tudor Revival on the intersection, this Italian Renaissance was built in 1931 by Chevrolet dealer A. J. and Mary Dow. Their daughter, Dorothy, traveled throughout Europe as an opera singer, until she returned home to give private lessons and serenade the neighborhood.

#43 Cedar Lawn Circle

Another entertainer of sorts, Balinese Room gambling don Sam Maceo built this home in 1950 when the family grew tired of living in hotels. He hired Frank Sinatra's Palm Springs architects Williams, Williams and Williams to design this California Contemporary, with interiors by T. H. Robsjohn-Gibbings of New York. Opposite a gated entry, the U-shaped open concept is strategically centered on four lots and hidden behind brick walls. Unfortunately, Maceo died before it was completed. His family moved to New Orleans in 1954, selling it to Jack S. Evans. In 1972, Robert L. Moody and wife Ann bought the old Maceo house, which has had several owners since.

#47 and #45 Cedar Lawn Circle

On your right, you'll see two early 1950s designs built one year apart for the same family. Designed by C. E. Stevens in 1953, the first house is a one-story red brick Ranch that was literally built by Roy Montgomery, Sr. The following year, he built his son and daughter-in-law a home of their own.

▶ **Cross South Drive, passing #18 on your right and #77 on your left; both will be included on your final walk in the District.**

#31 on the Circle

At the intersection of the Circle and South Drive, the Spanish Mediterranean was constructed in 1929 by dentist Dr. William H. Fletcher.

#34 Cedar Lawn Circle

Across the street you'll see a two-story Tudor home built by the superintendent of Galveston's Coca-Cola Company, Robert H. Maupin in 1927.

#38 Cedar Lawn Circle

This Georgian style home was designed by Ben Milan for furniture store owner Eddie Schreiber in 1938. Known as "Mr. Galveston," he served two terms as mayor, from 1960 to 1965. After the League of Women Voters, lead by Ruth Kempner, proved how corrupt the Commission form of city government had become, Schreiber helped change it to the mayor/council/city manager form. The tall red brick wall to your left is the back of Moody's compound at **#16 South Drive**.

#36 Cedar Lawn Circle

CEO of Gulf Coast Maritime Supply in Houston, Louis Druss built this Colonial Revival in 1948 for his first wife, Hilda. He sold the house in 1969 to Dr. Charles Borne, a neurosurgeon at UTMB.

#30 Cedar Lawn Circle

The dark red brick Tudor Revival next door seems to have been built by W. L. Moody III as a rental in 1928.

#26 Cedar Lawn Circle

#26 Cedar Lawn Circle

Catholic Bishop Christopher E. Byrne bought the lot from architect Clarence E. Stevens in 1947. He planned to build an Art Moderne home to be raffled off as a fund raiser for St. Mary's Hospital. Aline Mitchell won the house but sold it the following year to Loranzy Grillette, Maceo's "lieutenant" and manager of the Turf Athletic Club.

#20 on the Circle

Silas Ragsdale, publisher of the *Galveston Daily News*, built his handsome home in 1930.

#18 Cedar Lawn Circle

This two-story Tudor was built in 1928 by S. P. Mistrot, while next door Sam and Lena Braslau built their eclectic brick Tudor/Colonial Revival ten years later.

#15 Cedar Lawn Circle

Across the street, Mike Loomis bought this lot from the reluctant seller, Mary Moody Northen in 1947. Although designed by Stevens, both Mike and his wife, Helen, added their design ideas to this Art Moderne/Deco home. He then hired his brother's company, Gus Loomis Construction, to build it. Sitting on an oddly-shaped lot, note its numerous curves set against straight-edges, curved concrete steps and glass blocks at the entry.

#15 Cedar Lawn Circle

#14 on the Circle

At the intersection of Cedar Lawn Circle and South Drive stands a 1930 Spanish style built for Louis C. Elbert.

▶ **Cross South Drive.**

#12 Cedar Lawn Circle

Frank Boyd originally built a Tudor Revival here with one portico entrance in 1929. Grocer Jack S. Evans bought it and the lot next door in 1945, selling the property that same year to Trinity Episcopal Church for their rectory. Neo-Classical elements were added by Clyde and Fran Ellis in 1966 and the house continued to grow with subsequent owners.

#8 Cedar Lawn Circle

Owner of an Ice and Cold Storage Company, George W. Fraser built his Tudor Revival on two lots in 1929. With a total of 68 windows and a porte-cochere on its south side, the two-story tan brick features a balcony above its columned entry. In 1943, Fraser became Galveston's mayor for two terms.

#11 Cedar Lawn Circle

#11 Cedar Lawn Circle

Facing the entrance to Cedar Lawn, this two-story Spanish Colonial was built in 1926 for Dr. William E. Huddleston. Architect Andres Fraser covered the exterior with pink stucco, which the medical director for American National Insurance Company rejected. Huddleston hired contractor J. W. Woodruff to replace the stucco with tan brick, but the contractor refused. A law suit ensued. After a ruling and an appeal, the doctor finally won in 1934. Note its side yard that runs along South Drive.

#3 Cedar Lawn Circle

Built in 1953, this one-story red brick veneer home was constructed by Sydney Ory, an executive with the W. D. Haden Company. An engineer, it's thought that he designed his own house. Its double slab foundation is usually used in colder climates. The gable and columns are 1998 additions, giving it a Neo Classical style.

#6 Cedar Lawn Circle

Across the street, this California Ranch contemporary was designed by Ben Kotin for Ross J. Novelli and his wife, Pat. In 1969, they sold it to UTMB's Dr. Harry T. Hutchinson but bought the old Sam Maceo place at **#43** from the Moodys five years later.

#1 Cedar Lawn Circle

Contractor Ira C. Ellis built the only wood-frame home in Cedar Lawn in 1927. Called Dutch Colonial, this two story features a two Doric columns supporting its gabled entry porch.

You should find yourself back you car again after completing Cedar Lawn Circle. Drive around the Circle that you've just walked.

▶ 5 Park at the intersection of South Drive and the Circle in front of #14. On foot, turn right.

#1 South Drive

Behind #14 on the Circle stands this rather austere house, built in 1930 for the John Frenkel family.

#2 South Drive

Across the street, Gustav Kahn constructed this two-story brick Spanish home in 1929, valued at $25,000 during the Great Depression. "One of the most artistic of the homes in this section of the city," according to the *Galveston Daily News* on June 22, 1930, this brick Arts and Crafts "bungalow" featured tile detailing throughout the home—pastel in the bathroom. The Kahn family had arrived from Germany in June 1888. Two years later, baker Gustav established Kahn's confectionary shop with his brother, Emil, at 2107 Market, adding a wholesale ice cream factory. In 1920, Gustav Kahn partnered with J. M Levy to open a furniture store at 2117 Church. Kahn's widow sold their home to Dr. Edward Schwab, who sold it to Leo Shouldis,

#2 South Drive

owner of a New Orleans trucking company, in 1945. On the Island, he invested in Southern Select beer, two motels and the White Caps baseball team. Shouldis also bought the lot next door in 1951 and added a brick garage.

▶ ❻ Turn left, retracing your steps when you reach the fence.

#6 South Drive

Frank Prets built this small Classical Revival in 1948.

▶ Continue walking the South Drive by veering to the left; do not turn left at the Circle where you car is parked. You'll pass the expansive side yard of #11 Cedar Lawn Circle and see the back of #12 North Drive to the right.

#84 South Drive

Galveston architect Raymond Rapp designed this home for Joe Eiband, local dry-goods merchant, in 1950. The symmetrical late Georgian design, set behind a wide lawn of live oaks, lends an air of stateliness to the place. They had moved here from

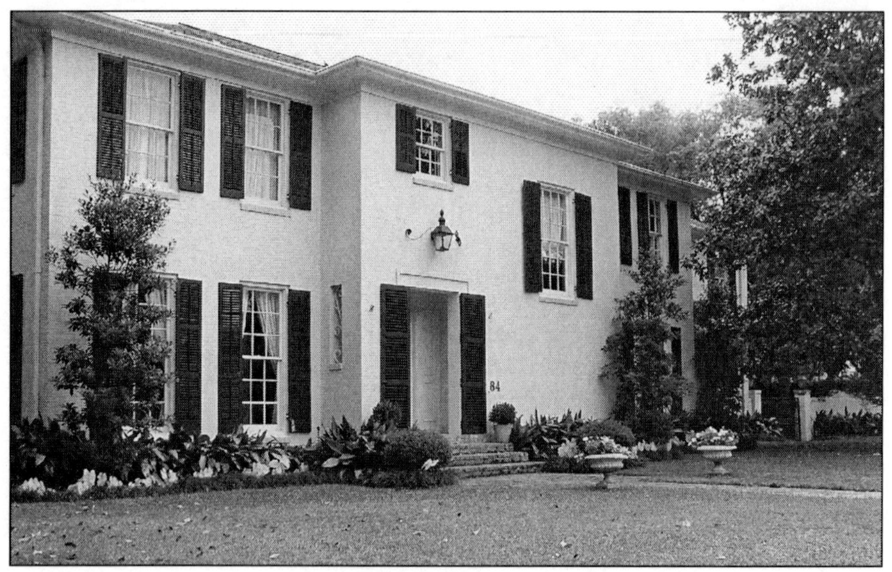

#84 South Drive

3118 Broadway, which Rapp had also designed for the family in 1928. Established by his father in 1936, Eiband's Department Store at 22nd and Postoffice, won acclaim as the most outstanding Department Store in the Southwest.

#16 South Drive

One of the founders of Cedar Lawn, W. L. Moody III, built this grand country estate on eight large lots, surrounded by an iron fence. The Neo-classical Georgian style home was built first in 1927, followed by the green house, swimming pool and bath house completed three years later. Robert Smallwood actually designed the compound, which fronts South Drive and backs upon the Circle, even though his boss, Alfred C. Finn, gets most of the credit. Note the large Corinthian columns at its entry. Moody left the Island in 1931, leaving the property to his brother, Shearn Sr., who died in 1936. His widow remarried, outliving her second husband too.

#77 South Drive

Former catcher for the New York Yankees, Homer Thompson, constructed this two-story red brick Georgian home in 1931. His wife, Lucy, was the granddaughter of Asa Griggs Candler,

#77 South Drive

who founded Coca Cola. They moved to Atlanta when Homer took a job with the parent company five years later.

▶ Cross Cedar Lawn Circle to complete the South Drive

#20 South Drive

#20 South Drive

Built in 1935, this brick home features a covered front porch trimmed with Spanish-influence archways. Mrs. Mary J. Hines was its first owner. Its neighbor to the north, a Classic Revival, was built one year earlier for the J. W. Hamptons.

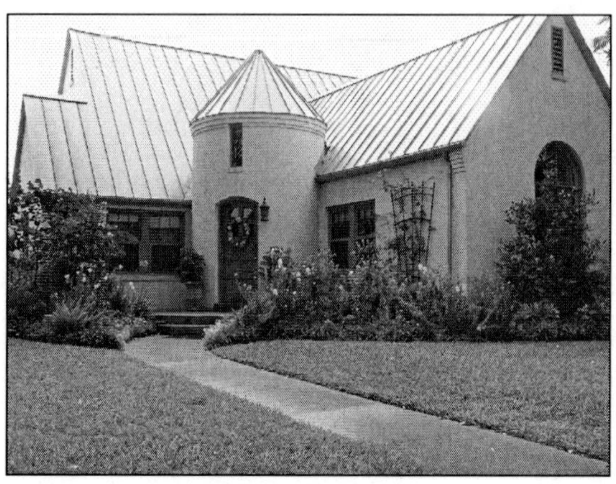
#24 South Drive

#24 South Drive

Cameron Fairchild designed this French eclectic cottage for real estate and insurance businessman, Edward R. Michaelis in 1931. Its inset Tudor-influenced tower with a steeply pitched roof creates a unique entryway surrounded by a lovely garden.

#40 South Drive

Across the drive, Alvin N. Kelso of the Texas Gulf Construction Company built this elegant Colonial Revival in 1948.

▶Ending your exploration of Cedar Lawn, retrace your steps back to your car on the South Drive, as these fabulous homes are certainly worth another view! Leaving this neighborhood by car, turn left on 45th Street.

4415 Avenue L

Note the original 1949 Spanish Mediterranean building of the first Spanish-speaking parish on Galveston Island: Our Lady of Guadalupe Catholic Church at the corner of 45th and Avenue L.

This concludes your walk of the two-neighborhood "Roarin' Twenties Realms" of the Denver Resurvey area: Denver Court and Cedar Lawn.

These are the fourth and fifth nationally recognized historic districts on Galveston Island, but there are others awaiting official recognition.

CHAPTER 8

Roaming the Kempner Park Neighborhood

South of Broadway on Rosenberg, distinctive brown street signs mark the eastern border of the Kempner Park Neighborhood, which takes its name from the city park at 27th and Avenue O. These signs are purely for decoration, however, as this variegated area has not begun the official process to be recognized as a historic district, either nationally or locally.

Rich in ethnic, economic and social diversity, original structures in this neighborhood include the oldest homes on the Island (dating to 1838), working class farms and plantations as well as 10-acre country estates of the wealthy and prominent City Fathers, in what has been called the "Villa District."

Although the the Kempner Park area extends westward to 37th Street, you will roam it only to 33rd Street, beginning with an illuminating walk in the Old Central/Carver Park area. Two African-American historical highlights stand on 27th St., at avenues L and M.

▶ **Driving east on Broadway, turn right on 27th Street. Drive 2 blocks south to Avenue L.**

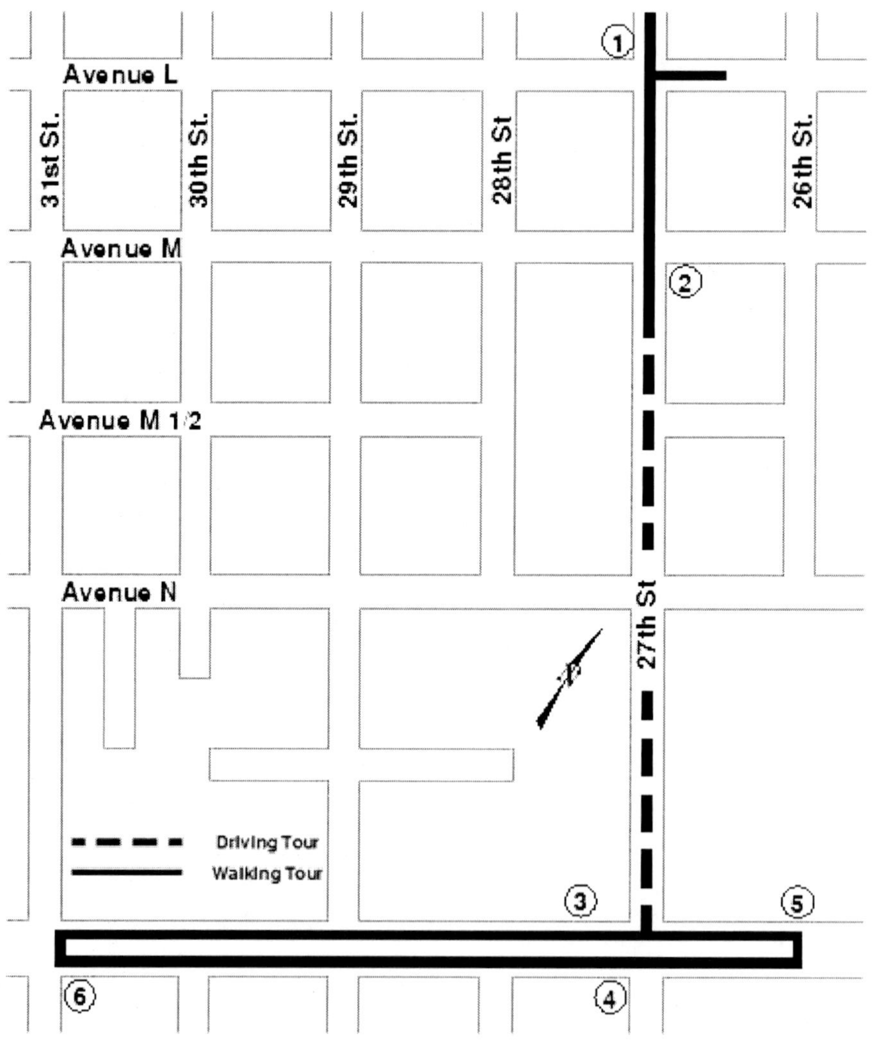

Kempner Park East

▶ ❶ Park. Cross 27th Street.

2612 Avenue L

Across a vacant lot, you'll see the side of the Avenue L Missionary Baptist Church, one of the oldest black congregations in Texas. The First Baptist Church, organized in 1840 by Rev. James Huchins, was the only white church to accept five slaves as members. This number grew quickly and, by 1847, split into the Colored Baptist Church, renamed the African Baptist Church two years later. Trustees Gail Borden, Jr., and John Sydnor bought this site specifically for their black slave membership in 1855. After the Civil War, the land was deeded to the First Regular Missionary Baptist Church. This 500 member congregation, under the direction of Rev. I. S. Campbell, built a brick church which was destroyed in the 1900 Storm. In 1903, they adopted the present name and constructed a small white frame church two years later. You'll see it standing behind the 1917 sanctuary. Designed and built by the African-American Tanner Brothers of Columbus, Texas, the present church features a vertical orientation with a tower at each corner, popular with southern black congregations from 1910 to 1950. Recently restored, note its stained glass windows. For a better look at the church, walk one-half block east.

▶ ❷ Retrace your steps to 27th Street and turn left, walking one block south to Avenue M.

2627 Avenue M

At the corner of 27th and Avenue M stands a relic from segregation. Behind the trees, notice the engraving carved in stone over the door: Colored Branch of the Rosenberg Library. Henry Rosenberg's estate left $400,000 to build a public library for all Galveston citizens, but when it opened in 1904, only whites were welcomed. A bill came before the Texas State Legislature to add an African American branch of the public library at an additional cost of $3,000. Located on this site, that branch was added to Nicholas Clayton's 1893 design of the all black Central High School. George B. Stowe's addition opened on January 11, 1905. Unfortunately, Clayton's design was demolished in the 1920s, so this addition is the oldest part of the complex, which now houses a cultural center.

▶ ❸ Turn left and retrace your steps one block north on 27th Street back to your car at Avenue L.

▶ Back in your car, drive south on 27th Street to Avenue O, a one-way street going west. Turn right, passing the Garten Verein. Turn right into the Kempner Park lot.

▶ ❹ Park your car next to the octagonal, multi-colored building. On foot, turn left and walk east, following the Kempner Park East map.

2704 Avenue O

This city park was originally the 10-acre suburban homestead, complete with plantation style house, of Robert Mills. Partner in the New York to New Orleans shipping company of Mills and MacDowell, he moved his business to Galveston in 1849 and established cotton and sugar plantations in Brazoria County. Once the state's leading entrepreneur and slaveholder, Mills used his ships for blockade-running during the Civil War, but was forced to declare bankruptcy in 1873.

Kempner Park Fountain
—From the author's collection

Three years later, a "band of finely nurtured Germans" (according to Julian Ralph in *Harper's Weekly*, 1895) formed a social club.

Purchasing Mills' estate, they built the wood stick Victorian Garten Verein Dancing Pavilion in 1879-1880. Based on an eight-sided style made popular by Orson Squire Fowler, who had visited the Island in 1859, the building was probably designed by German-born John Moser, although some attribute it to Nicholas Clayton. In 1896, an electric-powered fountain was added to the landscaped gardens, which featured a bowling alley, tennis courts and croquet.

When all things German became politically incorrect after World War I, Stanley Kempner bought the property in 1923 and gave it to the city as a public park in memory of his parents, Eliza Seinsheimer and Harris Kempner. That summer also witnessed the first production of the Little Theatre of Galveston at the Garten Verein. Then, as now, its poor acoustics are due to its top layer, which was added during the 1900 Storm repairs. Although still owned by the city, the pavilion is managed by the Galveston Historical Foundation.

Garten Verein Dancing Pavilion

—Courtesy of educator John Glen

▶ ❺ Cross Avenue O at the corner. Turn left and cross 27th St., walking east on the south side of the street.

2611 Avenue O

Raymond Rapp designed this late Mission Revival style home with California Hispanic influence for Sol L. Levy in 1923. The house features a central arched entry with a parapet, hollow tile roof and small porte cache to the east. Levy served as the Vice President and General Manager of Black Hardware Company for Houstonian Harry Black, who had bought the company from Ben Blum in 1910. It continued to operate on The Strand until the mid-1960s. Levy also built the house next door to the west four years later.

2603 Avenue O

Charles Fowler, Jr. hired C. D. Hill to build his understated home in 1917. Note how the shipping agent discreetly distinguished his house with a side hall entry topped by an elliptical fanlight, hedged fence and deep garden.

2523 Avenue O

The signal supervisor for the Gulf, Colorado and Santa Fe Railroad, Edward P. Hanson built this home in 1915.

2529 Avenue O

The house next door, also built in that year, was the home of dentist Dr. Alex A. Dyer. The Anglo-Palladian detail over its entry portico fancies this cubic house.

▶ ❻ Cross Avenue O. Turn left, walking back west on the north side of the street.

2504 Avenue O

Note the tall, stucco wall surrounding the Daniel Kempner Home which stands at the corner of 25th Street. The second son of Harris and Eliza Kempner, D. W. bought the north side of the two blocks between 25th and 27th streets on Avenue O from the Ursuline Sisters. Selling the rest to friends and family (and thereby assuring the quality of his neighborhood), he chose these three lots for his estate, designed by Mauran, Russell and Garden of St. Louis. Completed in 1910, it reflects a combination Spanish Colonial, Mission and Mediterranean styles. Kempner actively served on the boards of all the family businesses and also spearheaded the beachfront Hotel Galvez project in 1911.

2528 Avenue O

D. W.'s cousin, J. Fellman Seinsheimer, lived next door. The owner of the JMO Menard Insurance Company hired A. J. Bellis to design his home in 1914. His gabled Spanish Colonial incorporated the Victorian influence in its stained glass and central inside staircase. Its entrance columns are Italian Renaissance. Also set back behind a fence, Seinsheimer's home is approached by a circular drive, like a country estate.

2528 Avenue O

2602 Avenue O

Clothing manufacturer Samuel I. Miller purchased this lot from Kempner in 1913, and built his home two years later. Although unknown, the architect must have been influenced by Frank

Lloyd Wright in this definitive Prairie style, marked by its large square porch, horizontal orientation and low hipped roof. When the Millers moved to Houston in 1920, they sold the house to Heinrich Renfert, originally from Bremen, Germany. One of Galveston's cotton barons, Heinrich remarried after his first wife died suddenly in 1930. The new Mrs. Renfert commissioned John Staub to remodel the home three years later, enclosing the wraparound porch and adding a sunroom. UTMB Urologist Dr. Robert E. Cone bought the house in 1944. His widow lived here until her death in 1970. As you complete the block, note the 1915 Craftsman style at **2620 Avenue O**.

▶ **Cross 27th St., retracing your steps past the Garten Verein.**

2701, 2707 and 2709 Avenue O

Across the street on the corner stands the Steffens-Drewa House. Built in 1870 by Dr. Ferdinand Steffens for his wife Henrietta Luedeke, it originally faced east with the address 1703 27th Street. By 1873, Steffens added a rental house and office to the south on 27th Street. In 1891, his daughter Sofie married Edward F. Drewa, who used the family home to showcase his ornamental plasterwork. To its immediate west on Avenue O, the son-in-law built two raised cottages as rentals four years later, adding his trademark sunburst gingerbread in the gable of the peaked roof. Since Drewa had been associated with Alfred Muller early in his career, it is thought that this architect designed the two identical houses. The Drewa family kept these rentals until 1944.

When the corner house was raised in 1905, the son-in-law chose to rotate it 90 degrees to face Avenue O, creating quite a corner compound blending the Queen Anne and Gulf Coast styles. After Edward died in 1935, daughter Sedonia and husband, Paul Carder, moved in the corner house to care for her mother until she passed in 1948. The house did not leave the family until Sedonia died at the ripe-old age of 91 in 1982.

2816 Avenue O

Plantation owner and entrepreneur Robert Mills gave his niece,

Minnie Knox, the adjacent 2.3 acres of land to the corner of 29th Street when she married banker John H. Hutchings. They built their Greek Revival/Italianate villa in 1856, planting many live oak and palm trees which they named after family and friends. Nicholas Clayton was hired to repair the damage from an 1885 hurricane. Covering the original red brick with stucco, Clayton added a third story and two-story portico to its west side. Although the entrance remained on the south side, he replaced the two-story front gallery with a centered, single-story porch. Six years later, the classic revival had become a Romanesque Villa, inspiring the title "Villa District" from 27th to 35th streets on Avenue O. Hutchings died in 1906 and his widow followed eleven years later. Honorary Consul to Japan, J. H. Langben lived in the home from 1926 until his death in 1945, when Hutching's grandson, Sealy, purchased the property and restored the mansion and grounds. Upon his death in 1985, the home was bequeathed to the University of Texas Medical Branch. It debuted on the 1996 Galveston Historic Foundation's annual homes tour. The current owners fell in love with the Hutchings estate and moved to the Island, "breathing new life into an old home."

2816 Avenue O

Many of Galveston's prominent citizens, such as Menard, Mills, Hutchings and Ballingers, who lived on the large country estates in this neighborhood, intermarried with the Sealys, Moodys and others, creating various amalgamations of old Galveston names throughout the generations.

2805 Avenue O

On the south side of the street, George B. Stowe designed this house in 1896 for Hutching's son, Sealy, five years after he married Mary Moody, the daughter of Colonel Moody and sister to W. L., Jr. This two and one-half story Queen Anne features a wraparound porch on the first floor with Classical Revival details. In addition to banking, Sealy also ventured into the printing business with Clarke and Courts at 24th and Mechanic, while his wife raised seven children.

2827 Avenue O

Next door stands Raymond Rapp's Mediterranean style cubic house, built in 1925 for Dr. and Mrs. Wiley J. Jinkins.

▶ **Cross 29th Street.**

2901 Avenue O

The stately home on the opposite southwest corner was designed by Houston architect Cameron Fairchild in 1939 for lawyer Ballinger Mills, Jr. Paying tribute to John F. Staub's work, Fairchild incorporated the cast-iron balcony and front porch rail to add a Spanish Creole influence from the New Orleans French Quarter.

2908 Avenue O

The Texas Historical Commission plaque on the corner of the fence proclaims this site "The Cradle" because, in 1891, the "Daughters of the Republic of Texas" was born in the library of William P. and Holly Jack Ballinger's home. After the house was destroyed during the 1900 Storm, their grandson Ballinger built this home in 1911. Remodeled in 1922, this magnificent Georgian villa features a substantial gallery with arched openings and tan brick veneer topped by a green tile roof. Next door

2908 Avenue O

stands another Ballinger house, built for daughter-in-law, Carrie Mather, in 1900.

3006 Avenue O

Note how Congregation B'nai Israel Temple halts 30th Street on the north side of Avenue O. The congregation moved into this sprawling Ben J. Kotin design from its original 1860s temple on 22nd Street in 1955.

3028 Avenue O

On the corner, John E. Pearce replaced an 1887 Clayton home of the former State Attorney General R. V. Davison in 1915 with this C. D. Hill design. This cubic concrete house, with its horizontal orientation, features a wide front porch. Owner of a marine contracting and stevedoring company, Pearce served as Galveston's mayor during the Roarin' Twenties.

3102 Avenue O

Look across 31st Street to find the exclusive Galveston Artillery Club behind a tall, tree-covered chain-link fence. This first military company in the Republic of Texas was chartered in 1841 to protect the port and city. It reorganized as the Island's most prestigious social club in 1899. Moving from 1904 Seawall in

1955, their modern one-story clubhouse, designed by Thomas M. Price, still maintains the ambiance of old southern charm. The Galveston Artillery Club's lavish annual debutant ball remains the highlight of the social season.

▶ 7 Cross Avenue O and turn left, walking back east on the south side of the street.

1704, 1714, and 1724 31st Street

Oculist and Aurist Dr. Rolland C. Hodges bought this lot from H. M. Trueheart in October 1889, and contracted with August W. Bautsch to build a two-story shingle style frame house with a slate roof. Five years later, merchant Robert I. Cohen bought the home and added a large kitchen, extra bedrooms upstairs, and double galleries to both east and west sides. He also owned the two houses to the south on 31st Street, both built in the 1890s. Cohen's business was expanding too: from a small men's clothing store to a leading department store in 1906 to 1922. In 1917, he purchased the Foley Brothers Dry Goods Company, and son George moved to Houston to manage it.

3017 Avenue O

Behind the Cohens' corner home stands a large Queen Anne built by lawyer R. Waverly Smith upon his marriage to Jennie Sealy in 1897. While it was being built, the newlyweds lived in the old Sealy homestead, which stood at 23rd and Sealy. After mom Rebecca died, they chose to stay in the family home, living with her brother, John, Jr. The three of them founded John Sealy Hospital via the Sealy-Smith Foundation. This house became rental property until it sold to Henry Kirk Rowley of the Union Pacific Railroad in 1905. Designed by George B. Stowe, it features a one-story veranda and corner turret accented with a steeply pitched roof, reminiscent of those found in Galveston's East End.

3011 Avenue O

Next door is the 1899 home of Thomas L. Cross, a ship chandler, manufacturer's agent and commission merchant.

3001 Avenue O

Christian F. Hildenbrand arrived in Galveston from Germany in 1859 and established a sash, door and blind factory. After his death in 1889, his widow, Elsie, had this picturesque "shore-side" cottage built on property "to belong to her forever" in 1894. Two years later, she married bricklayer Otto Hoase who became the proprietor of Christian's company. Note the ample gingerbread on its five bays, the cobalt, yellow and cranberry glass in its transom and its two-tiered front staircase. In sharp contrast on the corner across 30th Street stands the somber, red brick home of contractor Walter A. Kelso, built in 1926.

3001 Avenue O

▶Continue walking east on the south side of Avenue O until you reach your car in the Kempner Park parking lot next to the Garten Verein.

▶Drive west on the one-way Avenue O to 33rd Street. Neither map reflects these driving instructions. On your way you'll pass:

3111 Avenue O

In the next block, across the street from the foliage-covered fence of the Galveston Artillery Club stands the Adrian Levy home Built in 1922 for the young attorney who would be mayor, this "pretentious stucco house" features a curved driveway to the front door. Levy hosted President Franklin D. Roosevelt here in 1937, introducing him to a young Lyndon B. Johnson.

3121 Avenue O

Down the block, you'll glimpse the 1872 B. F. Hutches home, an early southern townhouse with a fancy entry.

▶ **Turn right on 33rd Street at the light. Immediately after, you'll see a tall white fence on the left side of the street surrounding the Michael Menard Home. You'll find this route on the Kempner Park West map.**

▶ **❽ Park and cross the street to explore its grounds, if the gates are open. Note the monument.**

1605 33rd Street

Built on a 10-acre estate known as "The Oaks," the Menard Home is the oldest surviving building on Galveston Island. In 1838, a very simple four-room house/office was shipped from Maine. It is unclear whether Quebec-born "Michel" Menard or Augustus C. Allen—

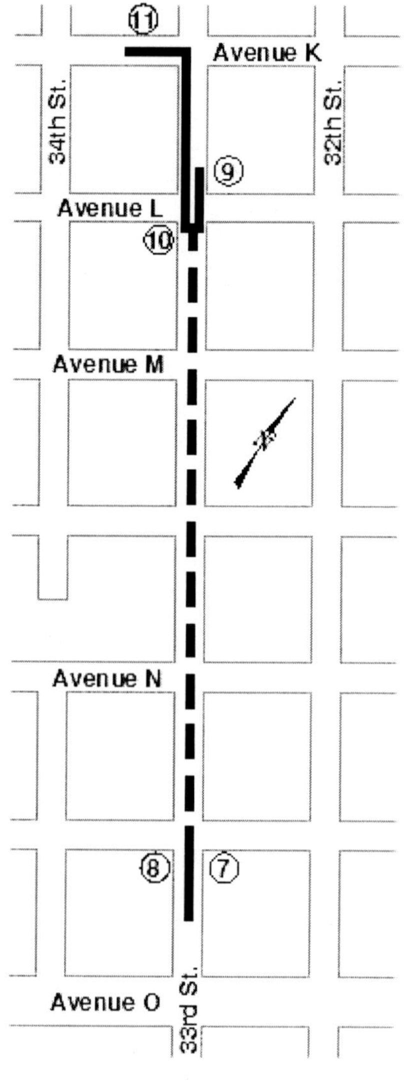

Kempner Park West

brother to John Kirby, who founded Houston—actually built it. Documentation proves that Menard bought it back from Allen in 1840 and remodeled it two years later into the grand Greek Revival mansion, complete with Ionic columns, that has been restored today.

Credited with founding the city in 1839, Menard formed the Galveston City Company with his partner, Thomas McKinney. They bought a "Labor and a League" of land on the Island's east end, but unlucky timing forced them to pay twice: first, in 1834, they paid $50,000 to the Republic of Mexico through their Mexican agent, Juan Seguin; then, two years later, they paid another $50,000 to the newly formed Republic of Texas for the same 4,605 acres. After the city's checkerboard grid was established, the Galveston City Company advertised its natural port in Europe, attracting such large numbers of immigrants that Galveston became known as the "Ellis Island of the West."

This home housed three of Menard's four wives, the second of which was his second cousin. He adopted the two daughters of his last wife, Rebecca Mary Bass, who outlived him and bore his only child—a son named Temple Doswell Menard, born in

1605 33rd Street

1850. The house also witnessed Galveston's first Mardi Gras Ball in 1856. Menard died later that year of blood poisoning and is buried in the Broadway Cemetery. His son sold the house to Captain Edwin Ketchum, who was Chief of Police during the 1900 Storm. It remained in the Ketchum family until 1977.

After several absentee owners, the Galveston Historical Foundation purchased the property in 1992. The current owners bought it two years later and completed its restoration in 1995, with the help of Rice University's architecture students. The 1838 "Michel" Menard Home is the only house on the Island to receive a first place award for exterior renovation from the National Trust for Historic Preservation. The Foundation manages the property, opening it regularly for tours and as rentals.

▶Back at your car, continue driving north on 33rd Street. At Avenue M, you'll pass into the Old Central/Carver Park District, which abuts the Kempner Park Neighborhood.

These two adjacent areas cover 748 acres, running from 26th to 54th Streets and along Avenue M across Broadway to Church and Mechanic. Although home to several early plantations, most of its residents provided longshoremen for Galveston's Port and other industrial and domestic labor.

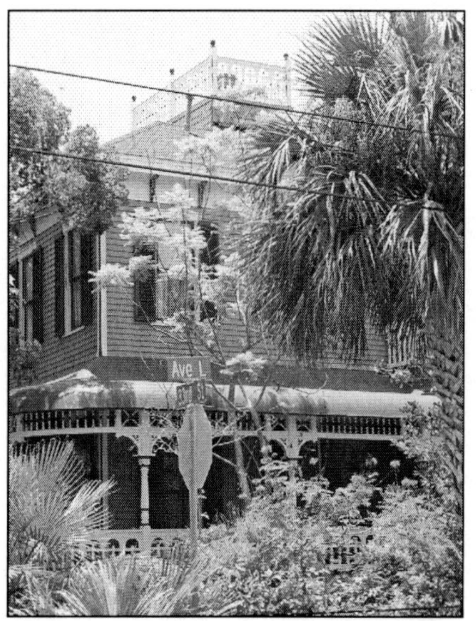

3301 Avenue L

▶ ❾ Park near the corner of Avenue L. Cross 33rd Street and walk the block between avenues L and K.

3301 Avenue L

With colorful Eastlake detailing, this elaborate Italianate/Queen Anne Villa was built in 1892 for produce commission merchant John Hagemann and his wife, Jerusha. Notice its wrap-around veranda, topped by a curved metal roof supported by shortened columns, and the widow's walk on the roof. City health inspector and head of the local Brewer's Union, Thomas Cobb bought the home in 1932.

▶ ⑩ Walk north on 33rd Street.

1121 33rd Street

Built by merchant/speculator, J. Myrant Smith in 1874, this Italinate sold to Mrs. John Sealy's sister, Mrs. Sarah C. Hartley, in 1881. She planted many mature live oaks on the property. Mr. and Mrs. Edward W. Goff owned the house from 1913 until they moved to Denver Court in 1930, when Frank C. McCoy bought it. His son Emmett remembered when his dad dismantled the original cupola so that he and his sister wouldn't fall off the roof. Frank and son expanded their small 1923 roofing company into the McCoy Building Supply Centers, now scattered throughout the state.

1103 33rd Street

A retired Confederate general, Lewis W. Carr, built this Doric-columned Greek Revival mansion in 1866. He sold it four years later to Richard Coke, who became the governor of Texas in 1874. Two years later, Horace and Julia Sloan bought it. In 1889, wholesale grocer Herman Marwitz gave it to his daughter Ida as a wedding gift when she married John Charles Gross. They expanded their honeymoon home. Nicholas Clayton designed the Queen Anne addition on

1103 33rd Street

the north side to include a ballroom, corner turret, and expansive bay window. An Arts and Crafts style rear wing was added in 1898. Turn left on Avenue K for a closer look. After the 1900 Storm, the mansion was raised eight feet, creating its impressive front staircase, guarded by two protective stone lions. The Gross family owned it through 1950, after which it served as both a church and a boarding house. The Carr-Gross Home suffered years of neglect until 1997 when this elegant mansion was restored to its original grandeur and opened as a Bed and Breakfast, surrounded by a lush tropical garden.

1019–21 33rd Street

Across the street, note the 1903 expansive Victorian cottage built for William J. Newcomb, an employee of the Galveston, Houston and Henderson railroad.

Looking west, you cannot help but notice the tall tower of St. Patrick's Catholic Church, which dominates the next block.

1013–27 34th Street

With the city moving west, Bishop Claude Dubuis established a Catholic parish between 34th and 35th streets one block south of Broadway in 1870, and named it after the patron saint of Ireland, St. Patrick. Founding member and Irishman Nicholas J. Clayton built a two-story frame church but, unfortunately, it was destroyed by a storm the night before the new pastor arrived from Indianola. With his small congregation, Father Lawrence Glynn picked up the pieces and started to rebuild with Clayton as the architect. On March 14, 1872, they laid the cornerstone for a massive 13th century Gothic Revival structure that would take 26 years to build. Father Glynn died on Good Friday, 1880, and was buried beneath the altar. The final phase was a 205 foot spire, topped by a Celtic cross, dedicated to the city's founder, Michael Menard. Unfortunately, during the 1900 Storm, that tower laid down backwards on the church, destroying the roof and interior. Talk about "the luck of the Irish!" Again, Clayton was chosen and St. Patrick's was rebuilt in 1905, just in time to raise it five feet to match the city's new grade level—the largest project of that nature in the city. The current tower, built in 1922, stands only 120 feet high.

Remodeled many times over the years, St. Patrick's celebrated its 125th Anniversary in 1995.

▶ ⑪ **Turn right twice to retrace your steps back to your car on 33rd Street. Now you have concluded your walk of the Kempner Park Neighborhood with a short diversion into Old Central/Carver Park.**

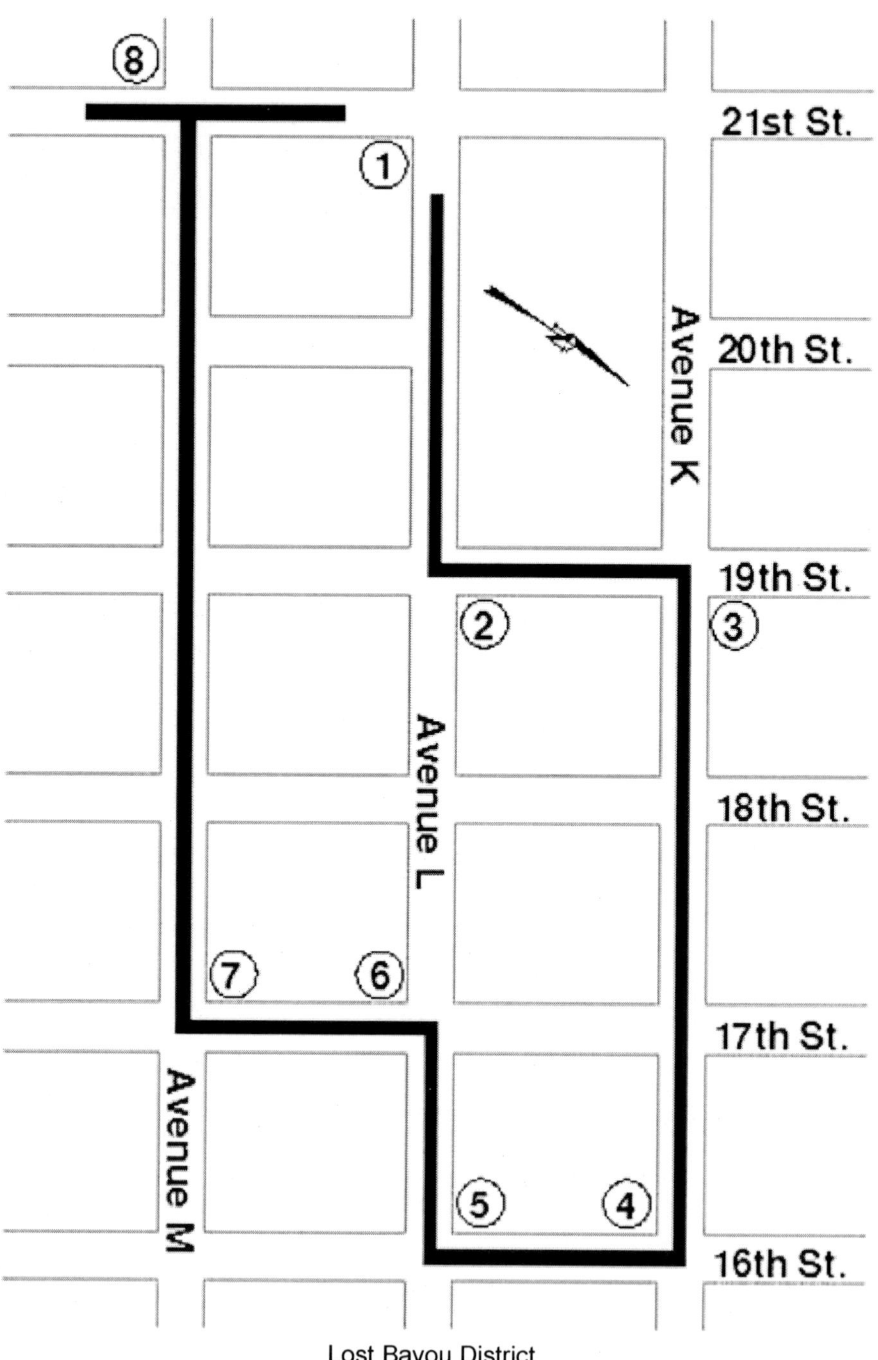

Lost Bayou District

CHAPTER 9

Lost Bayou District, Found

Within the San Jacinto Neighborhood

When the city was first conceived, south of Broadway was considered suburban and rural since it was so far from The Strand central business district. John D. Groesbeck platted larger lots and 10-acre outlots, each of which consisted of four regular city blocks. As the city spread southward, the area east of 23rd to 6th Streets slowly developed as a working-class neighborhood.

Over the years, its buildings fell victim to various disasters. Houses "curled up like burned paper," ravaged by the Great Fire of 1885, which jumped Broadway's wide boulevard at 17th, moved west to 21st Street and southward to Avenue O. Within a week, residents started rebuilding their modest middle-class homes with insurance money and low-interest loans. Although many were demolished during the 1900 Storm, the northwestern corner was spared by a wall of debris. Hurricane Carla, in 1961, spawned a tornado that cut a path down 23rd Street, before moving two blocks eastward.

On November 7, 1982, residents living in this widespread area christened it as the San Jacinto Neighborhood, naming it for the elementary school located on 21st Street, between avenues L and K. Originally organized and built in 1883 as the Avenue K or Second District School, it adopted the name of the famous 1836

Texas battlefield in 1905. In 1998, they planted a community garden at 2005 Avenue N ½, complete with one of Henry Rosenberg's restored fountains. The current association is beginning the process to protect its 1,200 historic structures through the city's local Landmark Commission. As a Neighborhood Conservation District, 51% of residents must agree to accept exterior guidelines for any new development to protect the historic character of their area.

However, those living from 21st to 16th streets and avenues K to M ½ within the San Jacinto Neighborhood organized their own historic district in 1994. The Lost Bayou Historic District took its name from Hitchcock's Bayou, a shallow lagoon that snaked inland from the Gulf of Mexico at 29th Street. Judge T. J. League took the lead by filling in this "mud pond" with beach sand in 1872. Messrs. Shields and Company actually did the work, which was completed just before the 1885 Fire.

The Lost Bayou District, that northwestern corner spared by the 1900 Storm, reflects the working class homes of the late 19th century. Residence styles include shotguns, bungalows and cottages, all incorporating the Gulf Coast influence. Although many of these houses are being restored, many more are waiting for rebirth by restoration, making this district a prime real estate investment! As the district's potential is achieved, more of their mysterious human stories will be uncovered.

▶ ❶ Park your car on Avenue L near the corner of 21st Street next to the first house.

1202 21st Street

Nicholas Clayton originally designed this raised "cottage" to face Avenue L in 1888 for real estate agent Gustave A. Meyer, who was from Germany. It appears that major modifications were made in 1933 by Dr. James A. Azar, which included repositioning it to face 21st, known as Center Street. However, its impressive gingerbread, dormered roof and double stairs at its entry still mark it as a Clayton design.

▶ Walk east down Avenue L.

This block faces the south side of San Jacinto Elementary School, which replaced an 1886 Clayton design after Hurricane Carla in 1961.

2009 Avenue L

George B. Stowe designed this house for A. H. Wainwright in 1899.

2001 Avenue L

Built in 1886 by Benard Levy, who co-owned a livery stable business, this house features a front bay window and double gallery under a peaked roof. One of his six children, Adrian Felix Levy, served as Galveston's mayor from 1935 to 1939.

1925 Avenue L

By far the most spectacular house on these two blocks, this home was rebuilt just after the 1885 Fire for George Schneider, a retired wine and liquor merchant. Dickey and Helmich designed the whimsical home with its mariner's wheel porch railing, accented by a creative paint job.

1925 Avenue L

1919 Avenue L

Title records seem to indicate that this house, a mixture of East Lake and Queen Anne styles, was built in 1887 for a Mr. S. A. Cook. Before the turn of the century, however, J. A. Theriot lived here. His widow sold it to Maude Brooks in 1941.

1911 Avenue L

This 1886 cottage features a decorative gingerbread inset just under the eaves of its gabled roof. Note its side dormer. The two houses on its left appear to be twins.

▶ ❷ Cross 19th Street and turn left, walking north on the east side of the street.

1126 19th Street

Currently a frame shop, this corner store formerly faced Ave. L. Louis Henry Defferari built it in 1886. He also owned its neighbor on Avenue L as well as the house next door at 1116 19th Street. After repairing storm damage, Defferari sold the store to the Deans in 1946.

1916 Avenue K

Looking west across the playground in the middle of the next block, you'll see a five-bay-wide (i.e., the number of sections across its front) home with a double veranda crowned at the center by a small peak. Dr. and Mrs. McKenzie Johnston built it after the 1885 Fire destroyed their original. Note its bay windows to the east and original iron fence.

▶ ❸ Cross Avenue K and turn right, walking east.

1828 Avenue K

In 1900, Mrs. Clara G. Batts built a tenant house at the corner of 19th and Avenue K. Note how its entry really fronts 19th Street more than the avenue.

1014 19th Street

Mrs. Batts lived in the home behind her rental on the alley, built 15 years earlier.

1814 Avenue K

Built in 1886 as a four-room cottage, owner James G. Seawell added a kitchen in 1897 while raising it eight feet. Facing foreclosure as three apartments in 1987, the Galveston Historical Foundation hired an architect to design its restoration. The current owners live upstairs, reserving downstairs for guests.

1810 Avenue K

Infant daughter Fannie inherited this property after her father was killed in a steamboat accident in 1860. Living at 17th and Market, she had the front part of this Greek Revival built as a rental in 1889. Eight years later, tailor Peter Nielsen had doubled its size, adding onto the back. The Henry Reybard family bought the home in 1911. Daughter Edith married the new architect in town, Raymond Rapp, and they lived here until his death in 1959. His widow sold it the next year.

1811 and 1805 Avenue K

Note the houses across the street. Originally built like the one on the right, the "twin" on the left was redesigned during the 1930s.

1808 Avenue K

William J. Killeen, bookkeeper for the Texas Cooperative Association, built this home in 1886. Dr. John Thomas Moore bought the two-story Victorian Greek Revival in 1899. Prominent physician Moore pioneered medical uses of radium.

▶ Cross 18th Street.

1721 Avenue K

On the large corner lot across the avenue, this house was built by the Devlin brothers in March 1886 for widow Agnes Erhard to replace one that burned during the Great Fire of 1885 that previous November. An Erhard family home after the 1900 Storm, both sisters and brothers are listed in residence at this address. Brothers Peter, Jr., and Bernhard partnered in a printing firm, perhaps started by their uncle, F. W. Erhard, who lived at 1620 Ball Avenue.

1717 Avenue K

Next door, George B. Stowe designed this two-story home to stand on 7½ foot brick piers in August, 1900, for port pilot Rucker T. Carroll. The next month, the Great Storm knocked it off its foundation. Other than that, the house survived with relatively little damage.

1720 Avenue K

Obscure insurance records indicate that this house was built in 1888 by a Mrs. H. G. Matilda Wagenbredt who promptly sold it to the Crofts and moved in with the Rakels on Postoffice Street.

1716 Avenue K

Originally built in 1888 for Alphonse Kennison, John Adriance, Jr., converted this house in 1897 to three apartments. He was a partner in the state's first real estate firm with its offices on 22nd Street just off The Strand. In December 1983, Galveston Historical Foundation records indicate that it was cited as a public nuisance due to an absentee owner in Connecticut. The Foundation bought the home from the Estate of H. T. Fountain and resold it to new owners.

1714 Avenue K

Adriance built this five-room bungalow as rental property in 1923. With its Craftsman exterior, its interior suggests more of a shotgun cottage in that it is only one room wide, with all others lined up back-to-back. The name of this Southern style comes from the implication that one could fire a shotgun through the

1716 and 1714 Avenue K

front door and out the back door without hitting any interior walls. When Adriance died that same year, his widow, who lived around the corner on Broadway in a Neoclassical mansion, sold this cottage to Samuel Fridner, who gave it to his married daughter, Rose Arnsfeld, in 1937. Austrian-born Aaron Farb bought the bungalow in 1952; he died here at the age of 99 in 1968.

1102 17th Street

Facing 17th Street set flush against the front sidewalk, this 1875 raised cottage was co-owned by molder Max Best and his brother, Charles. Note its two dormers. The house at **1106–08** was built in 1895.

▶ **Cross 17th Street.**

1615, 1617, and 1619 Avenue K

The homes on the south side of the street appear to be triplet designs, albeit modified over the years.

1614 Avenue K

1614 Avenue K

Designed in 1891 by British-born William H. Tyndall, Engine House #5 features arches over all front doors and windows. The two-story stucco-faced municipal building has recently been restored into a single-family home and art studio.

1605 Avenue K

The Galveston Historical Foundation bought this cottage from the First Presbyterian Church and moved it to this location from 19th Street, generating much interest during its restoration. The home sold quickly and the new owner is now finishing it.

1017 16th Street

For a closer look at the front of the next building, turn left and walk ½ block north on 16th Street. Prominent Galveston lawyer, Marcus C. McLemore, originally built this two-story Greek Revival wood frame home in 1870. At the entry, a two-sided staircase opened to its wrap-around veranda. The Society for the Help of Homeless Children bought it in 1901 to use as an orphanage. A partner with the Reymershoffers in the Texas Star Flour Mill, Morris Lasker donated funds in 1912 to enlarge the institution. Architect Donald N. McKenzie raised the building, expanded the basement and added an expansion across the back at the northwest corner. While the first floor, with its fifteen foot ceilings, was devoted to public communal areas, the second floor housed four dormitories with sleeping rooms for the matrons and attendants, "each with its own bathroom." The next year, the McLemore home was renamed the Lasker Home.

▶ ④ Retrace your steps and turn right on 16th Street to walk south.

1113–15 16th Street

The two-story on the alley was built in 1897.

▶ ⑤ Turn right on Avenue L.

1602, 1604, and 1606 Avenue L

The three two-story houses on this side of the street were originally built as one-story raised cottages, also in 1897. To accommodate more residents, the owners raised their outdoor basements high enough to enclose living space as the new ground floors. Note the unique sunburst gingerbread just below the roof on the corner house.

1607 Avenue L

Similar to those across the avenue, this 1890 house began as a 1½ story Colonial. After the 1900 Storm floated it from its foundations, its original ground floor was raised and a new one built in 1906. The home maintains is Colonial style by the four large columns on its double galleries. It now serves as a Bed and Breakfast.

While most of the houses on this block need restoration, their potential has been realized in the next blocks of this working-class neighborhood. On the northeast corner of 17th and Avenue L stands a tenant house built in 1883, a survivor of the Great Fire.

▶ ❻ Turn left at 17th St., walking south to Avenue M.

1207, 1209 and 1211 17th Street

Note the four shotgun cottages on the west side of 17th Street. Perhaps they may have been pre-fab commissary houses, which were used as emergency housing after the 1900 Storm.

▶ ❼ Turn right on Avenue M, walking on the north side of the avenue.

1713 Avenue M

Carpenter turned U. S. Custom House night inspector, Adolph Mennike built this cottage as rental property in 1887. Faced with a gable-fronted porch, it is relatively plain.

1714 Avenue M

This house was built the year after the 1900 Storm.

1717 Avenue M

In 1877, Mennike built this larger home for his family. Set on six-foot piers, it also has a gable-fronted porch, although much grander with its round inset beneath the peak. The steps originally paralleled the house on both sides of the door.

1725 Avenue M

Somewhat of a mystery house in its early history, this Greek Revival stands out because of its large corner lot, dormered roof and decorative gingerbread. The original story, listed by the Texas Historical Commission, claims that Delaware jeweler John Maxwell Jones built the home before 1867. His wife, Henrietta, was the daughter of French composer Jacques Offenbach. In addition to managing his shop named "#8 Strand," Jones helped organize the First National Bank of Galveston and took part in London's Crystal Palace exhibit in 1850. However, insurance records for this location indicate that watchmaker D. H. Pallais built the Gulf Coast cottage in 1878. Later owners include the city's benefactor, Henry Rosenberg, businessman Joe Levy and County Judge, E. B. Holman.

1725 Avenue M

1726-28 Avenue M

Known for his abundant gingerbread, Alfred Muller designed this 1888 home for Charles F. Rhode, who passed it on to his daughter, Edna Connor. R. H. Cobb bought the house after she died in 1944. Note its original double entry doors with a tran-

1728 Avenue M

som and the two carriage houses in the back. Originally from Krefeld, Germany, architect Muller graduated from the Royal Academy of Fine Arts in Berlin before moving to the island city in 1886. He lived at 2111 Avenue M ½ with his wife, the former Emilie Goldman, and 4 children.

▶ Cross 18th St., still walking on the north side of the avenue.

1801 Avenue M

Built in 1888 for Julia L. Spalding, this small 1888 three-bay-wide cottage combines Greek Revival with Queen Anne details. Its shuttered porch, facing 18th Street at the back, served a practical purpose as it provided privacy and protection from the elements. Although once very common on Galveston Island, extant examples are few.

1801 Avenue M

The home had a succession of owners over the years including Reagan and R. D. Campbell, a clerk for the shipping company, S. P. Atlantic S. S. Lines. Galveston Historical Foundation bought it in 1997. Ball High School students rehabilitated the home, under the supervision of GHF staffer, Jay Sims.

1806 Avenue M

Back on the north side of the street, this 1886 raised cottage was built for Benjamin F. Disbrow, a manufacturers' agent. Its simplicity indicates that it was a modification of larger Victorians with a projecting bay and recessed porch that made it more affordable.

1828 Avenue M

At the other end of this block on the corner stands the Sallie L. Shearer House. Built in 1891, she sold it 10 years later to attorney Marsene Johnson. Another Johnson attorney named Elmo lived here until Theophilus and Edna Webb bought the home. They added the kitchen and downstairs bathroom during the 1930s. C. E. McClelland of the American National Insurance Company then bought the house, which was used as a boarding house for military personnel during World War II. Restored in 2005, this high-raised double-galleried home features stick patterned gingerbread even on its west side entry porch.

▶ Cross 19th Street.

1904 Avenue M

This block of the Lost Bayou District abounds with two-storied Southern townhouses, a modification of the Greek Revival. Note their vertical orientation to enable them to fit on smaller lots. Contractor Robert Palliser bought two lots in 1895 from John Rogers and built this house for his own family that same year.

1905 Avenue M

The 1889 Robert Railton Home features a double entry door, complete with transom, and full-length windows that open onto both verandas.

1906 Avenue M

In 1886, Pallister built this Southern townhouse for John S. Rogers, insurance and loan man who invested in Galveston real estate.

1914 Avenue M

Alfred Muller designed this house in 1887 for Minnie and Howard Carnes. He was cashier for the Morgan steamship with "side wheel steamer packets" running regularly between Galveston, New Orleans and New York since 1858. When the Carnes' were transferred to Mexico in 1894, Irish coppersmith Paul Shean and his wife Bridget bought it. He owned the Paul Shean Plumbing and Manufacturing Company located at 2021–23 on The Strand. When he died in 1915, his daughter and son-in-law moved in. Joan and William Eichler lived here until 1962. Their estate sold the home three years later, with the proceeds going to Kirwin and Ursuline Academy. Complete with a turret, this Queen Anne features an arch motif throughout its façade. The 1887 Carnes house now serves as a Bed and Breakfast.

1914 Avenue M

1915 Avenue M

Across the avenue, Harris Kempner owned the original 1874 house on this site which was used as rental property. After it was destroyed in the 1885 fire, prominent attorney Walter Gresham built a simple three-room tenant cottage. Jacob and Adeline Singer bought it in 1895 from a Mr. J. S. Fountleroy. A Hungarian immigrant, Singer owned a book company that began publishing medical and scientific textbooks for the new University of Texas Medical Branch. They added a fourth room and modified the entry to a rectangular Greek Revival before the 1900 Storm. James E. Jackson lived here from 1906 until 1927 before he sold the cottage to John Orr. His widow, Edna, owned the home until 1983, when a new owner completed its restoration and added Caribbean landscaping for a distinctive Key West feel.

1920 Avenue M

Attorney Robert and Sarah Franklin hired Nathaniel Tobey to design this impressive double-galleried house in 1886. A hero in the Battle of Galveston on January 1, 1863, Franklin captured the Union spy, "Nicaragua" Smith. He also helped plan the Seawall after the 1900 Storm. Canadian-born John Wandless bought the house in 1931. He served with Gulf Coast security and intelligence while his wife, Vera, ran the British Allied and Merchant Navy Club. They received their U.S. Citizenship in 1950. Note the Italianate style double entry doors complete with transom.

1923 and 1927 Avenue M

From Gottingen, Germany, Adolph Flake immigrated to Galveston to join his brother Ferdinand in 1847, who published the *Union* and *Flake's Bulletin*. Adolph worked in his grocery, seed, imported wine and cigar business before he partnered with Lent M. Hitchcock to develop that Galveston county town. When his first wife died in 1882, Adolph married the younger Antoinette Biehler and bought a large home on this site which had once belonged to Marx and Kempner. Unfortunately, he lost that house in the 1885 Fire, but quickly rebuilt this cypress wood Italianate design that features a bay window. The house passed to his widow in 1892 as did the house next door, which she sold to Herbert L. Flake that same year. Both remained in the family, as rental property during World War II, before being restored in 1976. They are two of the few on Galveston Island to remain in the same family for over 100 years.

1923 Avenue M

1924 and 1928 Avenue M

Builder Christian Wolfer constructed these twin Victorian Gulf Coast cottages in 1894 as rental property. Their entry doors are framed above and alongside with small windows which may not be original.

▶Cross 20th Street, still walking west on the north side of the street.

2007 Avenue M

Across the avenue, lighter engineer George M. Prendergast built this two-story house, with its elaborate gingerbread, in 1886. To accommodate his family of eight, he added the double veranda during storm damage repairs in 1901. About that time, he received a promotion to dredge boat master.

2019 Avenue M

This raised shotgun was built in 1892 as one of many tenant houses owned by real estate developer, James M. Burroughs. "Wrecked" in the Great Storm, it was rebuilt in 1901.

2024 Avenue M

While its neighbor was built in 1888, this raised cottage wasn't constructed until after the turn of the century around 1907. The assistant Chief Clerk at the U.S. Engineers Office, Herman H. Gold only lived here for three years before he moved to San Antonio. He sold the home to S. E. Slaughter, who owned a typewriter and stenographer company. The house features original transoms above the doors, which are still working.

▶Cross Avenue M.

1302–04 21st Street

Built in 1891, this two-story home was originally built as a corner grocery store. It was remodeled by the Ivey family four times over the years: in 1912, 1915, 1922, and 1945, to serve as apartments. Widow Annie Ivey sold it to Moris Ofman in 1956. He converted the downstairs into a furniture repair shop. The house now serves as an art studio and gallery.

1306 21st Street

Charles L. Flake built the house next door in 1891.

▶Cross 21st Street for a closer look at the Galveston Orphanage through the live oak trees, palms and oleanders.

1315 21st Street

George and Mary Ann Dealey from Liverpool, England, founded the Island City Protestant Orphans Asylum on October 20, 1878. A Board of Directors chartered the children's home as the Galveston Orphans Home in 1880 and, with funds received from donation boxes scattered throughout the city, bought the property at 21st and Avenue M nine years later. The Dealey family moved to Dallas that same year, where their sons became the editor and publisher of the *Dallas Morning News*. Philanthropist Henry Rosenberg died in 1893, leaving $30,000 in his estate to build a permanent home. A new Gothic Revival building was officially christened the Galveston Orphans Home on November 16, 1896.

Although architect Alfred Muller had guaranteed that it would "last for generations to come," the 1900 Storm collapsed its middle. It may have been his last design as he succumbed to typhoid that same year.

Six weeks later, William Randolph Hearst sponsored a benefit at the Waldorf Astoria in New York City to raise money for a new orphanage on the Island. Its headliner was Mark Twain. Another $30,000 funded the present Orphans Home, designed by George Stowe, which he proclaimed as "eclectic Renaissance Revival." Dedicated on March 25, 1902, this massive brick and stone estate featured larger dormitories for all and three "fine fireplaces." One faces "the main entrance on Center Street, another in the reception room and a third in the dining room," as reported in the *Galveston Daily News* two days later. Closing as an orphanage in 1983, the building was restored as a single-family dwelling five years later and renamed "Tavilleh," but it still sports the cornerstone of Muller's 1896 Gothic Revival building.

▶ 8 Turn right to walk back to your car at the corner of Avenue L on 21st Street On your way, you'll pass the following.

1214 21st Street

This house was built in 1913 by H. G. Schaper. His widow, Mildred Louise, sold it to Rosalie Mazzara in 1949.

1127 21st Street

The last house on your walk of the Lost Bayou District is across 21st Street, catty-cornered from your car. Carpenter William Pautsch built this "simple one-and-one-half story frame, shingle roofed cottage . . . containing two rooms" as probably the first of three lakeside homes on Hitchcock Bayou in 1867. A bridge crossed this intersection of Center Street and Avenue L. In 1905, Pautsch sold it to real estate investor, Timothy Sullivan. The cottage was raised and a new ground story added, complete with columns across the front gallery, prior to 1912.

This concludes your final journey of Galveston's historic neighborhoods as listed in this guide book, *Walking Historic Galveston*. Please don't hesitate to explore the city's vintage sites, again and again.

Appendix

An immigration Port of Entry since 1825, Galveston saw thousands come through to its natural harbor in search of freedom, land and business opportunities. As early as 1840, the Island's community affirmed a truly diverse citizenry, with members of every nation living and working side by side. Their occupations also varied greatly: from risk-taking entrepreneurs to the bookkeepers who worked for them; world-renowned doctors and clergymen; sea captains, grocers and gamblers; saloon keepers and weathermen; craftsmen, commission agents and cotton factors. The city thrived, as its port served the growing Southwest as the center of a commodity business that even a Civil War didn't stop.

Living sophisticated lifestyles, the more affluent entrepreneurs celebrated their success by building elegant homes, grand entertainment venues and impressive office buildings. Those employed by the prosperous also benefited, enjoying the Island's cosmopolitan atmosphere and gentle breezes from the Gulf of Mexico. The center of trade, finance and culture in Texas, Galveston was the largest city in the state for almost twenty years.

The Great 1900 Storm

Galveston stood at the height of prosperity and promise as the second wealthiest city in the United States based on per capita income at the turn of the twentieth century. Ironically, the powerful source of its prosperity—the surrounding sea—would reclaim much of its own.

On Saturday, September 8, this barrier island served her geological purpose, suffering the worst of the "Greatest Natural Disaster to Hit the United States" Within fifteen hours, the city's promising future sank, swallowed by a 16-foot wall of water that attacked from all sides—gulf, port and bayous. Meteorologist Isaac Cline clocked the winds at 120 miles-per-hour until his gauge blew away at 2:30 in the afternoon, and the worst of the storm happened after dark. Fully one-third of the most populous part of Galveston Island was literally swept clean, leaving 6,000—perhaps as many as 10,000—people dead. That next Sunday morning, while most survivors were dazed by the destruction, eight affluent city fathers organized the Central Relief Committee to insure the city's survival. With the help of Clara Barton, aged president of the American National Red Cross, the crisis was averted. Galveston's long recovery had begun by the end of the year, but the storm took its toll on the Island's prosperity, forever changing the course of its destiny and making it *The Galveston That Was*.

Howard Barnstone's book, published for The Houston Museum of Fine Arts in 1966 opened with an enlightening quotation, in which Edna Ferber likened the city to a Charles Dickens character:

"Yet the city had a ghostly charm . . . The houses, potmarked by salt mist and sun and heat and mildew, seemed to be built of ashes. Here was a remnant of haunted beauty—gray, shrouded, crumbling . . . (resembling) Miss Haversham . . . the spectral bride in *Great Expectations*."

A Kind of Magic

To defy nature or perhaps to spite the "Powers That Be," insightful city fathers that year chose to build the city's future on its past, perhaps prompted by Barnstone's book. The era of urban renewal that swept over the nation post-World War II skipped over Galveston, leaving the city's 19th and early 20th centuries' structures standing, but greatly dilapidated. Funded by the Moody Foundation, the Kempner Fund and private donations, the Historic American Buildings Survey through the U.S. Parks and Wildlife Department hired architect, John C. Garner, Jr., in July 1966 to conduct an investigation into the restoration potential of Galveston's historic structures.

A Texas-born "authority on 19th century architecture," he conducted a block-by-block investigation of the eastern third of the city in October to list its viable and valuable historic buildings. Galveston's was the "first large-scale effort to focus community attention" toward "a unified effort in preserving and protecting" its historical heritage as a way to enrich "the appeal of sun and sea in holding visitors." Coincidently, the U.S. Congress mandated a historic preservation program for the nation at the same time.

From his initial Galveston Architecture Inventory of 1,000 buildings, Garner discovered a great number of significant structures standing throughout the city that reflected every stage and age of its development. From the mansions to shot-gun houses; an opera house, warehouses, boarding houses and row houses; cottages to office buildings, fountains and statues, even a dancing pavilion, barracks and a bordello—all were deemed worth the time, trouble and expense to restore for generations to come.

To further position Galveston Island at the forefront of the historic preservation movement, Garner launched a grassroots PR campaign for historic preservation in 1967. From local groups to national politicians, he appealed to all, stating that the Island city had the "wealth and will" to protect its historic treasures for the future. His campaign reached its pinnacle when Secretary of the Interior Stewart Udall came to town on February 18. Amazed at the rich history he found here, he stated, "You have something future generations will praise you for preserving." Even Governor John Connally noted the positive "relationship between the preserved past and the profitable present." Oh, their prophetic words. . . .

Garner then issued a mandate for the Galveston Historical Foundation to establish a Historic District Plan as their priority project. This became part of the Foundation's mission: "stabilization of older neighborhoods into safe and attractive places to invest." The first two areas to be recognized were the central business district and the residential east end.

He also suggested inexpensive booklets of historic areas with guided tours of the districts and properties by specially trained, knowledgeable tour guides, urging cooperation between all levels of governmental entities, business investors and historical societies involved.

Under the leadership of Peter Brink, the non-profit organization took control of every aspect of historical preservation in Galveston:

funding avenues and information, maintaining a list of historical properties for sale and guidelines for restoration, investing in historic properties to resell, offering practical workshops on restoration techniques and salvage warehouses, even courting wealthy "IBCs" (i.e., Islanders By Choice) to buy and restore historic properties.

The results stand on the eastern third of the Island, ours to explore and enjoy.

Bibliography

"1880 Garten Verein." City of Galveston and Galveston Historical Foundation. n.d.

"A Brief History of St. Patrick Church." n.p. 1997.

"A Riding and Walking Tour of a Residential Community Listed in the National Register of Historic Places." East End Historical District Association. Various n.d. revisions.

Barnstone, Howard. *The Galveston That Was*. Houston: Rice University Press, 1966, 1993.

Beasley, Ellen and Stephen Fox. *Galveston Architecture Guidebook*. Houston: Rice University Press, 1996.

Cartwright, Gary. *Galveston: A History of the Island*. New York: Atheneum, Macmillan Publishing Company, 1991.

City of Galveston Historic Districts. Galveston: Department of Planning and Community Development. n.p. 2002.

Davis, Albert B., Jr. "Galveston's Bulwark Against the Sea: History of the Galveston Sea Wall." U.S. Corps of Engineers. Presentation made at the Second Annual Conference on Coastal Engineering, 1951.

"Drive Out Today to Beautiful Cedar Lawn, Galveston's Beauty Spot." 75th Anniversary Booklet. Cedar Lawn Association. n.p. 2002.

Eisenhour, Virginia. *The Strand of Galveston*. Self-published. 1973.

Fox, Stephen. *The Grand American Avenue*, Chapter 8: "Broadway Galveston, Texas." Rohnert Park, CA: Pomegranate ArtBooks, 1994, pages 207-229.

Galveston Historical Foundation Resource Center, 1861 Custom House, 502 20th Street, Galveston, Texas 77550. Archival Materials.

Galveston Historical Foundation's Informational Plaques in the Downtown Historic District.

Galveston Historic Homes Tour Brochures. Galveston Historical Foundation. n.p. 1974-2008.

Galveston Daily News. Various articles, 1850–1967.

Handbook of Texas Online. Austin: Texas State Historical Association. http://www.txha.utexas.edu/handbook/online/articles.

Harris Garden, a project of the Galveston Foundation. Interview with John Campbell, January 2007.

Hyman, Harold M. *Oleander Odyssey: The Kempners of Galveston, Texas, 1854–1980s*. College Station: Texas A&M University Press, 1990.

Leavenworth, Geoffrey. *Historic Galveston*. Houston: Herring Press, 1985.

Lienhard, John H. "The Engines of Our Ingenuity: Episode 1099: Robert's Rules of Order." Houston: University of Houston, KUHF Radio, 1996.

Lykes, Mrs. Genevieve Parkhill. *Gift of Heritage*. n.p. 1969, pages 68-137.

McComb, David G. *Galveston: A History*. Austin: University of Texas Press, 1986.

Miller, Ray. *Ray Miller's Galveston*. Austin: Capital Printing, 1983.

National Register of Historic Places Online. Washington, D.C.: National Park Service. http://www.nps.gov/history/nr.

Nesbitt, Robert A. "The Legend of Nicholas Clayton." Port of Galveston: Presentation to Texas Historical Society. n.p. 1974.

"Old Red: Ashbel Smith Building." Galveston: The University of Texas Medical Branch. 1988. Online Revisions.

Rosenberg Library's Galveston and Texas History Center, 2310 Sealy, Galveston, Texas, 77550. Archival Materials.

Scardino, Barrie and Drexel Turner. *Clayton's Galveston: The Architecture of Nicholas J. Clayton and His Contemporaries*. College Station: Texas A&M University Press, 2000.

"Self-Guided Walking Tour." Silk Stocking National Historic District Neighborhood Association. n.d.

Texas Heroes Monument Commission, 1989 Restoration. n.p.

Texas magazine, *Houston Chronicle*. "Corners of the Past." September 19, 1999.

THC Atlas Online. Austin: Texas Historical Commission. http://atlas.thc.state.tx.us.

The Moody Mansion and Museum. Mary Moody Northen, Inc. n.p. 1991.

"Walking Guide, Strand National Landmark District." Galveston Historical Foundation, 1984 and Revisions.

"U. S. Appraiser's Building" Exhibit Brochure. n.d.

About the Author

Fifth generation Galvestonian **JAN JOHNSON** has been seriously studying the Island's rich history as a part-time Tour Guide since 1982. A direct descendant of two 1900 Storm survivors, her interest in her Island heritage was born when her mother, Dorris Stechmann Johnson, became secretary to John Garner's Historic American Buildings Survey in 1966-67.

Jan earned a Bachelor of Science in Elementary Education at the University of Houston in 1986 with a 3.94 GPA. In 1995, she attained her Masters of Art in Literature when she researched and wrote the history of Galveston's Little Theatre, 1922-1942. She took the full time "free fall with free lancing" in May 2000.

Her stories have been published in various local publications such as *WHEREHouston*, the *Galveston County Daily News*, *Twisted Parrot*, *OutSmart* and on Guidry news Service. In September 2004, Jan completed more scholarly research on "The Reymershoffers: Early Texas Czech Entrepreneurs" for the Czechoslovak Genealogical Society International's newsletter, *Nase rodin*.

Walking Historic Galveston: A Guide to Its Neighborhoods is her first book. Based on her driving tours, this practical guide offers walker-friendly routes of the Island's most concentrated historic areas with interesting anecdotes about the people of their past.